CICELY BERRY

from word to play

A handbook for directors

WITH A FOREWORD BY MICHAEL BOYD
Artistic Director of the Royal Shakespeare Company

OBERON BOOKS

LONDON

First published in 2008 by Oberon Books

521 Caledonian Road, London N7 9RH

Tel: 020 7607 3637 / Fax: 020 7607 3629

e-mail: info@oberonbooks.com / www.oberonbooks.com

CONTENTS

FOREWORD

IT'S MY GREAT GOOD fortune to have worked at the Royal
Shakespeare Company while Cis Berry has been at play. Her guid-
ance and her lobbying have been crucial to the best successes of
the RSC in recent years.

Her creative impulse, like Shakespeare's, is born out of paradox:
the more familiar she has become with her material, the more
prepared she is to hurl it into the anarchic air of her rehearsal room.
The ruthless rigour of her approach to Shakespeare is matched only
by her subversive disdain for received ideas. Her founding role in
the tradition of modern voice teaching gives her the freedom to
embrace the new-minted with open arms. Above all, her achieve-
ment has been to rubbish the meaningless opposition of thought
and physicality; of mind and body, teaching us instead to embody
thought in rigorous and responsible childlike play.

And that is the spirit that has informed this book, her latest
contribution to our efforts to make theatre an ever more powerful
voice, fit to express the greatest human stories for the twenty-first
century.

Michael Boyd
Artistic Director
Royal Shakespeare Company

INTRODUCTION

I HAVE CALLED this book *From Word to Play*, but equally I could have called it *From Play to Word* – or just *Word Play*: for it is simply about raising our awareness to this wonderful, but subliminal, connection between the meaning of the words we use, and their sound and the physical movement involved in making them. This happens as we speak in everyday life as well as in the written text, for every word is an action.

I want to say here, right at the beginning, that this book is about releasing both the actors' and the directors' subconscious response to the sound of the text, and through that response to find a deeper and 'other' layer to its literal, surface meaning. In doing this we have to take on board that there is still that primal need within the listener for a cadence and a rhythm which will move us – whether it be to laughter or to tears. This book, however, is not about making the text sound 'beautiful'; rather, it is about allowing that essential connection between the meaning and the sound to be heard and to impact on the hearer in all its variability and its roughness.

We will be looking closely at this interchange between the sound and rhythm in language, and how that sound and that rhythm can:

   i change the nuance of the meaning,

   ii affect our instinctive emotional response, and

   iii take us into that 'other' world – ie, the world of the play.

There is a mystery in every play that is written, no matter whether classical and poetic or modern and demotic, and it is the sound and the rhythm of the writing which take us there.

So why am I writing this book? When a group of actors and a director first get together to work on a play, depending on the director's preference, they may do one of a number of things – here are a few examples:

i   They may spend time reading the play round the table, discussing meaning, objectives, relationships, etc.

ii They may put aside the text and explore the story through improvisation.

iii They may delve into their own personal lives in order to find their own connections with the characters.

iv They may work through movement and mime.

There are many strategies or methods which a director will use, all of which can be immensely creative and imaginative and not necessarily language-based, yet they are all finding ways to unfold their understanding of the story. This 'understanding' involves a literal perspective – for example, why and how things happen. I am after something different: I want us to engage in our subconscious response to the language itself and hear where that takes us, how it enriches both our understanding of the character and the world of that character, and ultimately how that enriched understanding reaches and engages the ear of the listener.

What seems to me so extraordinary about dramatic writing is that the writer is setting down, on paper, words that they hear the character speaking. They are not setting down a series of logical sentences, they are setting down the rhythm of another person's thoughts and how they knock against each other: it is through that rhythm that the character emerges. Thus it is the purity of that rhythm and those thoughts that we have to capture, without overloading it with our own meaning and our own feeling.

In my last two books, *The Actor and the Text* and *Text in Action*, I have set out the work which I have been able to develop over the years. This is work which I believe in, and I have very few new approaches or exercises to set down. However, since writing them I have become more deeply focused on the rehearsal process itself:

INTRODUCTION

I am convinced that this work on language, both hearing it and feeling it physically within our bodies, should become integral to this process, for it will give us a heightened understanding of the play itself. Here in this book I will try to show how this can be organised: how the work on language, and our response to it, can be layered through the rehearsal process in whatever form that is taking.

Edward Bond always says that the actor needs to feel the language in the body, and I think we should never forget that language, wherever it originated, started as noises expressing a need, a feeling, an intent, whether of anger or frustration or desire, to another living being; and that noise, that sound, that rhythm, came from the body as a whole. The sounds were obviously tempered by climate, space and distance, developing over hundreds of thousands of years into forms of words, or grammar, giving it specific meaning – ie, language. But how many thousands of languages? We should also be aware that speaking is in itself a positive, if not aggressive, act, for simply by making sound we are asserting our presence. This means that however offbeat and 'cool' the style of the writing, the actor has to be specific to that 'cool': it can never be just thrown away, for the listener must be allowed to pick it up. It requires skill to be both offbeat and yet present in the word.

Even now we must not forget that sound and rhythm have a very basic – I would say primal – effect on us, and we do not quite know why. We can be moved by the sound of someone's voice and are drawn in to listen – there is something in the vibration that attracts us. The sound of the words themselves also affects us: those words expressing a harshness of feeling so often have a grating or sharp sound, whilst those meant to comfort are smooth and more soft, and these sounds land on us quite unconsciously and affect our reaction.

The rhythm of the language also conveys the mood very strongly: specific rhythms can make us sad, but they can also evoke laughter. I have written about this in *Text in Action* and because I think it is so important I will repeat the story I wrote about comedy rhythm.[1]

---

1   For the full story, see *Text in Action* (Virgin Publishing Ltd: London, 2001), 18.

Johnny Beattie, the well-known Scottish stand-up comedian, came to a workshop that I was leading on *King Lear*. It concentrated on my own production of the play – one of the last plays to be put on at The Other Place, the old tin hut which was the RSC's original studio theatre – in which his daughter, Maureen Beattie, played Cordelia. Now Johnny Beattie had seen little Shakespeare, but as we worked through the scenes between Lear and the Fool he was astonished, for as he listened to the lines in the text the Fool uses as he tries to get a laugh out of Lear, he recognised them as being in the same rhythms as those he uses now to get a laugh from his audience today – three and a half centuries later. I think this tells us something quite central to our reaction to language: that the rhythm of language affects us in a very deep way, and that we understand something through that rhythm which may be outside our full literal comprehension. Think how often we have laughed at a comic dialogue in Shakespeare, or any other classical text, without fully understanding the underlying argument – one by Touchstone or Feste, for example. For me, this was a very important discovery, for I think it has a deeply profound message for us now as we bring Shakespeare into the 21st century. For it is more than just about speaking the text of a play, it tells us something about our innate reaction to the rhythm of language as we speak, and how that rhythm has a direct effect on us.

We can be deeply moved by certain rhythms, and the way the music of a speech can build and take us with it. The speeches of Winston Churchill and Martin Luther King were examples of this – unfortunately, so were those of Hitler. The whole art of rhetoric, first recognised and developed by the Greeks, has built up over thousands of years: how certain forms of speech, linked with rhythm and cadence, can evoke specific responses in the listener. These rhythms in speech can inspire, calm, or incite to violence, and it is the rhythm itself which affects something deep inside us, not necessarily the argument. Patently this can be dangerous. We do now of course have the 'soundbite', but I have a feeling that that is not here to stay for it does not satisfy the ear's need for music, and therefore does not engage with our feelings. Perhaps it is because

4

of this that our response to it is so often cynical. Conversely, is it the prevailing mood of cynicism that has brought in the soundbite? We, as humans, long for something to believe in: perhaps that is the bottom line.

I endorse very strongly that this sense of cadence and rhythm in the language, however minimal, is of primal importance to the way the actor works, be it for classical or for modern text, heightened or demotic. As Edward Bond has said to me, the actor must listen to what the character is telling them, and they must hear that through the movement of the language. Of course all the research into character, meaning and situation has to go on as before; but the specific work on hearing where the text takes us should be continually layered through the rehearsal period, for it both enriches and opens up the meaning, and in the end it will not only grab the listener's attention, but it will take the actor themselves into that deeper truth within. This in itself is an art.

I want to set out in this book a way of organising the work on language in order that it can be fully integrated into the rehearsal process – I will not go so far as to call it a 'method', for that word has so many overtones and implies a didacticism which I cannot go along with. To me the work is of vital importance and integral to the full understanding of the play being rehearsed, for it subtly takes our response away from the mind and roots the words in our whole self.

But I want to do more than this: I want to challenge the way we approach a play. I want to go as far as to ask – can we do Shakespeare any more in the west? Do we really hear it any more? Have we become too bound by reading about the text, the references and glossaries and all the possible meanings, that we have lost touch with the language itself, and it ceases to resonate within us? Because a play is set down in writing we think we can interpret it by understanding it literally. We then proceed to find a concept for it, we place it in a set, we get the characters to move in order to tell the story clearly and give it its dynamic. However, in doing this we so often lose the dynamic of the language itself and its centre, for words are as much an action as crossing the stage. Also, because Shakespeare's writing is our literary heritage, we too often feel we have to honour its literary status, thus forgetting that all the heat in the language, the coarseness, the violence, the passion, the sorrow, came out of a very basic sense of survival. I so often feel we have lost its roughness, and therefore we lose the immediacy of its impact – its basic reality.

This book is about taking us back to that reality: I want to put the exercises I have developed into a context that can be used during the rehearsal of a play, and in training work. However minimal the language, it is that language which takes us into the world of the play and the world of the character. The thoughts are at the centre.

In our analytical study of dramatic literature we have stopped hearing its sound – I would say we have lost our innocence. We should not allow academic analysis to be rated more highly than an intuitive understanding of the sound of the language. I would like to quote here two sentences from Walter J Ong's book *Orality and Literacy*. It is an extraordinary book which sets out to explore the differences between oral and written culture. It gives me particular pleasure because it sets the sound of language in its proper place – ie, as part of its deep intellectual content, and not as something which can be enjoyed if you happen to be inclined that way. The two sentences are as follows:

> In a deep sense language, articulated sound, is paramount.
> Not only communication, but thought itself relates in an alto-
> gether special way to sound.[1]

This tallies with my long-held belief that we do not, we cannot, understand Shakespeare in all its complexity fully, or indeed any dramatic writing however extravagant or minimal, until we have spoken it aloud and heard where the sound takes us. By that word 'sound' I do not mean anything extravagant or overdone, I simply mean that the sound, the movement of language, and its very thought structure must be felt in the body, or we will not get to the

---

1   Walter J Ong, *Orality and Literacy* (Routledge: London, 2002), 7.

centre of the play. I hope the work set out in this book will help to get us there. In real life the sound alters us as we speak: each word is an action, both in terms of the movement in the mouth, and in terms of our decision to speak; it is the same for any character in any play.

I want to say that although my focus is on Shakespeare, because that has always been the bottom line of my work, the exercises and strategies I am going to list are for all texts, both classical and modern, and will hopefully enlighten their meaning whatever the period of the writing: I will include examples of modern text as we work through.

The centre of this book, then, is Chapter Five (page 105), for in it I have listed all the rehearsal strategies which I have developed over the years in order to free the actor's response to the language itself and discover other possibilities – I like to call them 'diversion' or 'displacement' strategies. These are strategies which, by taking the conscious mind off the literal need to make sense, allow the words to be on the moment and to surprise. For me they are of basic importance, for they allow the words to take us into that other world – the world of the play. That world belongs to us all.

One further word: I think it is difficult giving a name to those who work on voice in a theatre company. The terms that are used – 'coach' or 'teacher' – I think narrow its field down, for they are not necessarily teaching the actor how to speak the text, or correcting what they are already doing: rather, they are opening out the possibilities in that text and letting the actor connect with them in their own way. It is a very creative job. I may be alone in this, for my colleagues may not necessarily agree, but I will henceforth be referring to them as the 'Voice person' – not necessarily satisfactory, but the best I can do for the moment.

SECTION ONE
The Work and its Roots

Chapter One

HEARING LANGUAGE

A Global View

THERE ARE NOW roughly six thousand languages spoken across the world. By the end of this century it is estimated by linguists that probably only about three thousand will have survived. I learned this from Mark Abley's book *Spoken Here*,[1] in which he tells of languages in many parts of the world which are at risk of being lost: it is tragic to think of just how much oral literature is being lost to the world. However, the languages which dominate the media will live on, English being one.

English, or should I say forms of English, is certain to survive, for it is the language of the global market place: it is the language of techno-speak and business jargon and text messaging. I think it is possible that Chinese, in whatever form, may come close to English's dominance because of its financial reach; it might even take over, but it does not have that imaginative language of street-cred and rap. However, what is important for us to understand is this: once we lose a language we lose the idiomatic expressions of that place to which it belongs, and so we lose the living essence of its culture. As Sello Maake Ka-Ncube, the great South African actor whose first language is Zulu, said to me one day: 'Each language has its own way of naming the world'. I find that both precise and deeply moving. How often do we remember what our mother or grandmother used to say and, in so doing, how that other world and

---

1   Mark Abley, *Spoken Here: Travels Among Threatened Languages* (First Mariner Books: Boston and New York, 2005).

that other time comes alive, and we feel it as a part of us; and that is merely our own culture. We therefore have to ask two questions:

   i The essence of just how many cultures are we going to lose?

   ii How are we naming our own culture?

So English will survive, as I have said, but at what price and how will it change? Will it be reduced to the language of facts, of lists, of organisation, of balancing accounts, of making laws – and of being in charge: all the practical issues which relate to things as they are, the facts, and which are dealt with by the left side of the brain? This will lead to over-simplification and a narrowness of understanding, because everything has to be quantified, named and listed, so the finer points are too often left out. It also leads to difficulties at work where rules of management give precise guidelines as to the procedures which must be followed, but with no allowance for the vagaries of the individual, the subtle variations within seemingly similar situations, and the differences between people – their *humanness*, in other words. But what of that other language, the language of the imagination, of telling stories, of wrestling with ideas and feelings – the language of real communication, of people wanting to talk about the issues which concern them and their community, issues of conscience, of ideas, of dreams? Even texting by mobile phone cannot fulfil this deeper need to communicate! Surely it is this language of real exchange which needs to be fostered, indeed *must* be fostered – and where better to do this than in the theatre?

   In 1999 I read by chance a review of the book *The Alphabet Versus the Goddess* by Leonard Shlain,[1] and it sounded so interesting that I immediately went out and bought it. It is so lucky that I did, for it has changed my mindset and judgement on so many things in small ways – how people express themselves in different situations, how they react to changes round them, and how they react to each other, and it has very subtly changed how I think. But above all it has changed my perspectives on language, how we read it, how we speak it and how we hear it.

---

1 Leonard Shlain, *The Alphabet Versus the Goddess: The Conflict Between Word and Image* (Viking: New York, 1998).

The book's thesis is both very simple and very profound. It sets out to prove that it was not until the first alphabet (possibly Sumerian) was formed that women lost their power – in fact they ceased to become goddesses. It tells how the man, who was the hunter/provider, saw straight ahead, while the woman, being the nurturer/gatherer, had a more inclusive view of the world, and of space. The man saw the space ahead of him while the woman saw the space around her, and this profoundly changed both their perception of reality, and the way they communicated. Now when an alphabet was formed people were able to set down facts in a precise order and quantify them, and this was attractive to the male, being the hunter who saw straight in front: the list was set down for good and could no longer be changed. But the implications were far-reaching, for it also meant that when a story was written down it could no longer be changed in the telling – it was there written in text. Of course this changed the whole nature of story-telling, for when you *read* a story the facts remain absolute, but when you *tell* a story the imagination is involved and the story can change slightly just by the words that are used, and how the memory, and the bias or subconscious preference of the teller, tilts it. Facts involve the left side of the brain: imagination, memory, seeing pictures, involves the right side.

It becomes clear then that the alphabet, because it could set down things in a straight, linear way, became the favoured way of recording details of lineage, of codes of conduct, and of history – it became the male prerogative. Whereas the woman – because of her many and varied duties connected to family welfare and nurture, which were too complex to be recorded – found it simpler, and perhaps more practical, to rely on oral communication. So the left side and the right side of the brain were no longer in agreement, with the result that women, although they had a possibly fuller and richer understanding of the community of which they were part, no longer held the same power. Laws were written down and had to be obeyed, and it is precisely because they were written down that they had that extra validation and authority. They became the expression of the male ruler – male supremacy: thus the woman,

12

who was still embedded in an oral culture, and despite her extraordinary practical abilities, became secondary. It is extraordinary to think of the alphabet as the great divider.

Now of course this division of man and woman is no longer applicable in the same way, although it is still a very complex area and varies greatly between cultures. In Great Britain, as in the rest of Europe, women are extensively involved in law, in administration and executive positions, as well as making a significant contribution to our literary heritage – both past and present. Yet there is still great complexity regarding areas of male and female equality and duty. But as I have said, English will survive as a global language, a language of the market-place with its techno-speak, business jargon and text-messaging – this language of the left side of the brain, the language of order, of making categories, a language which does not address those issues which have no concrete answer. It is the language of the organiser who cannot understand – or does not want to understand – human complexity and divergence because it cannot be set down. Perhaps that is why, as I have already said, so often simple problems in an organisation take so long to get solved, and why experts in 'people management' have to be called in at great expense. It is also intermixed with gender and the issues to which that gives rise, for there is no room for human manoeuvre.

Our Primal Need for Theatre

But of course this other language will continue, the language of the right side of the brain, for there will always be novelists, poets, poets of rap, idealists and writers of dreams, but – and this is what is important – we must never allow it to become secondary. I believe this is where theatre plays such a valuable and necessary role in our culture today, for it can take people into that other world, it can plug into our imagination and, most important, it can provoke us and make us want to talk, to discuss, to think – to communicate through language. It can make us question not only our beliefs and the way we live, it can make us question ourselves. And surely this primal need to exchange ideas and desires is basic to our sense of community – if we still have one. I know I have quoted this line from Thomas Kyd's play *The Spanish Tragedy* elsewhere, but here it is again for I think it has indeed become the touchstone of my work:

Where words prevaile not, violence prevailes.[1]

Some while ago I was in Brixton Prison taking a workshop with Bruce Wall's wonderful initiative, The Dream Factory. The group was working on scenes from *The Winter's Tale*, and I have seldom heard Leontes' speeches – language of great complexity and imagination, expressing such depths of disgust and jealousy – spoken with such a sense of ownership of the text. There was a real physical involvement with the language, and such evident pleasure in the release of thought and feeling through those exact words. That is perhaps an extreme example, because of course for them there was a sense of freedom, if only briefly, from the rigours of prison life. However, it was yet another proof to me that this rich, complex and extravagant language, which plumbs the very depth of human feelings, be they good or bad, speaks in a very particular way to us all, regardless of education or reading ability. Those men experienced both satisfaction and pleasure in speaking that language, and through that experience they found a confidence, which in turn made them want to talk and discuss the play itself: in other words, they were thinking creatively. I believe then that the actor has a particularly important part to play in our community, for it is his or her job to release us through the text into that other world, and to excite us with its sound and sense and, most important, to make us aware of the real and ever-subtle power of language. When you read you are concerned with the meaning of the words on the page: when you tell, other parts of your consciousness come into play. The literal meaning is only a part of the whole; the actor has to deal with the whole.

I am very concerned by the fact that because some people naturally have a quicker reading skill than others, they are deemed to be

---

1   Thomas Kyd, *The Spanish Tragedy*, Act Two Scene One.

more intelligent: does this mean then that those who have greater opportunities for reading as a child, or those who have an initial facility with the alphabet, those with the greater left-side brain power, get the better start? This is an unnerving thought.

The Actor's Skill

So, for theatre to exercise its full impact the actor needs to engage the audience: he or she needs to provoke and excite people with the need for language in order to wrestle with ideas and feelings and make them want to talk. The language can be poetic or rough, stylised or offbeat, but it must impact on the hearer in a positive way.

It is therefore essential that we both recognise and respect the range of skill the actor needs. I think that the actor's job today is a continual balancing act which requires practice and time, for it must take into account the heightened and the rough, the poetic and the demotic, the extravagant and the minimal: it is a skill that we need to be aware of, and practise, and never take for granted. It always has been difficult, but I think it is particularly so now when working classical text, and this is for a variety of reasons.

Firstly, we must not forget that fashions of language, the way we speak and the word patterns we use, are forever changing: if you hear a newscast of ten years ago, for example, it sounds dated. Now if the actor is working on heightened and poetic text they have to honour the size of that language and its imagery, yet we do not want a sung, slightly old-fashioned 'poetic' sound for it must seem to be spoken as of today, here and now, or it loses its potency and therefore its relevance to us now. Yet at the same time that text, be it Shakespeare or Marlowe, Jonson or Massinger, or any of the great Jacobean playwrights, is dealing with big issues both personal and societal, 'earth-shifts' as Edward Bond would call them, and the images used to express them are equally extravagant; yet the actor has somehow to fulfil the size of those images, make us experience them in a personal way, whilst keeping them real and specific and of the moment. But there is more to it than that, for there is something in the very music and rhythm of that language which of itself is moving, and which transmits the essence of the thought and of the play. This music, this rhythm has to drop into the ear of the listener so that its effect is both felt and understood. The actor therefore needs to become sensitive to the needs of the listener and aware of those moments necessary for the thought to drop in, and also aware of those slight lifts of cadence which increase the intensity of the thought and move us into another area of interest – you could say, heat us up. The bottom line is this: we still have a primal response to the sound of language, its rhythm and its cadence, and this sound has to be honoured for it carries its own truth, yet it has to equate with the sound of today – a very subtle balance.

Conversely, if the actor is working on modern text, quite downbeat and vernacular, where size of feeling is conveyed minimally, the actor is again walking a tightrope for he or she has to convey the underlying nuances, tensions, depth of feelings, the cost to the character, without in any way losing the offbeat nature of the writing. In whatever space, the language must be so precise as to convey the world of the play and the size of the feelings in a quite minimal way – and so often this happens in the spaces between the words, and the specificity of the word itself, for no other word will do. The text must impinge on the listener's consciousness without seeming to, but it can never be 'throwaway', for the choice of language is always specific, it is always meant, and must always lie on the ear of the hearer. If the character is 'cool' we must understand the reason for that 'cool'. It is so important to remember that within the rhythm of a section of text, be it prose or poetry, there will always be spaces – ie, moments where the sound, the meaning, can drop into the ear of the listener. This is not a pause, it is simply a moment of suspense between words or thoughts: Edith Evans used to call it a 'poise'. I think that expresses it beautifully, for it does not in any way hold up the line, rather it subtly creates in the listener a sense of suspense and of wanting to hear more. It lets the idea lay so that we are ready for the next with greater speed; the moment of poise does not hold us up: rather, it allows us to gather speed afterwards.

This also makes us aware of how the poet or playwright must hear the language in their head, for the rhythm and phrasing are integral to the sense. Not long ago an actor came to me because he was having difficulty in rehearsal: he was working on a new play which was being directed by the writer herself. The work was broken up in lines of equal length so it was not prose, neither was it verse because it did not have a specific pattern of rhythm: yet the line lengths and the punctuation were specific to the meaning of the play. By going through the text, finding the spaces between the punctuation, and the spaces at the end of each line, he found a meaning, a mood, which informed his character: but he had to let go of his literal interpretation to find that other meaning and that other place. Similarly with a very powerful new play *trade*, by the black writer debbie tucker green, the meaning was conveyed in the thought rhythms. The play looks at sex tourism through the stories of three women who are each involved unknowingly with the same man. The writing is dense, subliminal, fast and like a poem, with the exact pauses written, and the actor has to be able to honour the speed of the writing and its rhythm, yet lay the argument of the play precisely, for each of its sections takes us to a different layer of experience which the hearer has to follow. It is a tough challenge and requires a very subtle spacing of the words and how they take us on a journey through the different layers of the story. I believe this sense of the space in language is of the essence.

For the writer, the essence of the meaning is locked in the rhythm – whether smooth or broken, it is in the length of the phrases and how they knock against each other – be it Shakespeare or Rudkin, Jonson or Pinter, Massinger or Beckett. Meaning is rhythm, and rhythm is meaning. I believe strongly that we need to put time aside during rehearsal to heighten our sensibility to the sound and rhythm of the language, to each other and to how we respond. For we all speak differently, we all hear differently, and that is as it should be, yet there is a rhythm, a music, however minimal, which is intrinsic to the writing and which we have to carry through together.

So could this be a different way round for the actor, a different way of entering the character? It is about first listening to what the character is telling you, listening with purity to the words, before creating the story that you think the character is living, before coming to conclusions. We need to take time to listen. But I also think that because we have been ruled by an accepted standard of speech for so long, a 'received' pronunciation, and although we have now left that behind – and indeed much drama is written in dialect – there is still something inside us which is afraid of letting go; there is still that subconscious feeling that there is a 'right' way of speaking, and I believe this makes us wary of becoming directly involved with the words themselves. But this we will go into later.

Another part of the juggling act is speed. Now speed is a very important issue for, as humans, we think very fast, so the listeners' minds need to be fed at a fast rate, but it is how the actor manages that speed which is crucial. It is particularly important in classical text where the thoughts are so often long and convoluted, and it is only by giving the whole thought in one arc that it will be comprehensible to the listener. We must remember that Shakespeare did talk about 'the two-hour traffic of our stage'. The director will therefore demand speed, and rightly, but because we live in a literate culture we think that speed is about getting to the end of a phrase or sentence or speech as quickly as possible so that the literal sense is kept intact; but this is literate speed, not oral speed. In other words we are speaking the text in clumps of sense, which prevents us from discovering the word at the moment of speaking, the thought in action, and allowing for those moments of finding or dwelling on a word – those moments of 'poise' which make the listener hungry for what is to follow. This tends to make us cut the syllables down to the same length so that the varying lengths and textures of the words cannot be discerned. It is the same with dialogue: the actor is so often put under pressure to pick up the cue quickly, and this leads them to respond before the words spoken to him or her have dropped in, so that they are not responding to the actual words spoken but rather to their overall sense, and this inevitably leads to a generalised and prethought response – they are too 'ready'. The words are not allowed to take us to that 'other place', and therefore the language is not active and does not excite as it should.

For the actor, then, it is this speed of thought in all its infinite variability that has to be caught and transmitted; but for the director it is very different. The director chooses to work a play because he or she is excited by the story, what it says, how it can be presented and because it will provide an opportunity to present something which has not been expressed in that way before – an opportunity to create a new piece of theatre, be it classical or more modern. However, because the director reads it, and gets an idea about it and how it should be presented, the need to make it exciting forces him or her to make decisions on so many issues before being confronted with the actors. In today's world this is often unavoidable, but it makes it all the more essential that the actors are given the time to come to the text in their own way, and without too much preconditioning. Of course the director will need to give them the basic concept and context as he or she sees it, but the way the actor finds the language for themselves, be it extravagant or minimal, has to be a creative process for each actor, and time has to be given for this as part of the rehearsal process. Language written has to be found.

As I have already said, when working on classical text, particularly Shakespeare, we have lost our innocence. We come to the plays with too much information. In Shakespeare's day probably only eight per cent of his audience were literate – they came to listen, perhaps for the first time. They laughed because the correspondence between sound and meaning was funny. They cried because the sound and the meaning reached them in a different way, evoking other emotional reactions. They did not come to appreciate, to hear what the actor would 'do' with the part, to see how the director put it into context – to 'see' the play – they came to listen to the story and to be involved actively in the telling of it.

Now there is nothing we can do about this, for we read Shakespeare at school and we know the stories and we bring all the baggage – academic information, reviews of past productions – so that it is a great deal more difficult for the actor to get to the audience in a fresh way, to make them see it and feel it anew. What the actor has to do, therefore, is be specific to the thought, to allow one thought to provoke the next, and so keep it in the moment: this will make us hear it afresh. It may also surprise us. I love the fact that in the early nineteenth century Shakespeare was the favourite entertainment of the gold miners in the west of America. What is amazing is that all his stories, and the stories of those Elizabethan and Jacobean writers, still have so much to say that fuses with and informs the modern world.

One of the central issues for the actor today is emotion and how we deal with it. In this we have been heavily influenced by American 'Method' work – their take on the teaching of Stanislavsky, which leads the actor to believe that they are not giving their best unless they are demonstrating the emotion and filling the words with feeling. We cannot but be affected by what we see on television and film where the feeling is so often there on the surface and apparent. So when it comes to the powerful emotions of Shakespeare or any classical text, the tendency is to swamp the language with emotion without allowing the thought to impact or, crucially, to be surprised by it. But if the thought does not come through with clarity we lose the reason for the feeling, and this leads to generalisation, a wash of sentimentality: as I believe sentimentality to be the prerogative of the rich, this should be avoided at all costs because it cheapens the issues at stake. Now of course the emotion is there, but it is only when you have found and expressed your thoughts that the emotion takes over.

Language, expressing thoughts, is always about the need to live through those thoughts – and win: in other words we speak to survive. To quote Edgar in *King Lear* (IV i) –

> The worst is not,
> So long as we can say 'This is the worst'.

I suppose the question that forever intrigues me when working on a play is – where does that language come from? Does the writer think what they want to say in those lines and work it out grammatically, or do they come from somewhere else in his or her consciousness – an extraordinary crystallisation of thoughts? There is of course no answer, but it is intriguing all the same to realise that character, meaning, rhythm and image are intertwined so closely. How else could Beckett write –

KRAPP: Past midnight. Never knew such silence. The earth might be uninhabited.[1]

– so that we experience through the rhythm and the image something of that sense of Krapp's desolation. Or Williams –

BLANCHE: I shall die of eating an unwashed grape one day out on the ocean.[2]

– so we realise the total absence of reality inside Blanche's mind. Or Bond –

LEAR: (*Looking in the mirror.*) Who shut that animal in that cage? Let it out. Have you seen its face behind the bars? There's a poor animal with blood on its head and tears running down its face.[3]

– so we are taken into Lear's mad world. Or Shakespeare –

JULIET: Gallop apace, you fiery-footed steeds,
           Towards Phoebus' lodging![4]

– so we can inhabit and capture the sexual longing of Juliet as if inside her mind. Or –

LEONTES: Inch-thick, knee-deep, o'er head and ears a fork'd one![5]

– so we experience the physical hurt and violence of Leontes' jealousy. Or –

---

1   Samuel Beckett, *Krapp's Last Tape.*
2   Tennessee Williams, *A Streetcar Named Desire,* Scene 11.
3   Edward Bond, *Lear,* Act Two Scene One. (see page 69).
4   *Romeo and Juliet,* III ii (see page 96).
5   *The Winter's Tale,* I ii (see page 64).

BRUTUS: And therefore think him as a serpent's egg
           Which, hatched, would, as his kind, grow mischievous,
           And kill him in the shell.[1]

– where, through the image of a serpent's egg, we are let into the covert nature of Brutus' thoughts.

In all these instances the image is not just descriptive, it is of paramount importance because it is where the character is living at that moment; and the actor has to take us there. Edward Bond says: 'You write with your voice'.

I came across a letter the other day from Peter Brook, and I think it makes the perfect starting point for this book. Several years ago I organised a conference of Theatre Voice people from all parts of the world to meet and discuss the speaking of classical text in theatre now, and give their views on training. I invited Peter to give the opening talk. He sent me a letter to say that unfortunately he had other work on hand, but that if he had been able to come he would have said something like this – and I quote:

> Once upon a time Shakespearean sound was no more than
> a marvellously rich, resonant sound, with only generalised
> content. Then as a reaction there came a second phase.
> Here was a new interest. This was focused on a more precise
> content – but still linked to a very detailed observing of the
> musical rules of verse – the conscious observing of feet,
> beats, breaks, stops etc.
>
> However, today, this too is out of date. It produces what to
> our ears is still that artificial, self-consciousness that is the
> hallmark of the 'well-trained British actor'.
>
> We are ready for another revolution. To my mind, the new
> direction – deeply influenced by a century of close-ups – is
> the purifying of thought. This comes about by a long weigh-
> ing and tasting of the words and their sequences, that is
> never separated from – on the contrary, rigorously related to

---

1 *Julius Caesar,* II i (see page 116).

– levels of meaning. Only when the thought pattern gradu-
ally becomes clear can a new level of fresh, ever-changing
impulses inform the words. The thought brings with it the
feeling that in turn makes the word-patterns. These – through
being cleared of encumbrances – become in their very nature
musical. This music is free from all the old rules. It is a
natural music, rediscovered each time.

As always, cogent and at the nub of the argument – and very gener-
ous. 'The thought brings with it the feeling that in turn makes the
word patterns' – this must surely be the key rule for the actor today.
The work that follows in this book I hope both clarifies this and
makes it possible.

Lastly I would say this: because the actor always feels under pressure to convey all the meanings, nuances, feelings of the story,
the tendency is to over-fill the language with intentions. Trust the
language, give it its right weight, and keep it simple. Listening is a
collective act between the actor, the text and the audience.

Chapter Two

LAYING OUT THE WORK

Where the Work Began

I WANT TO START by saying a little about the work itself and how it has evolved through the years. It is the work that I have been able to develop over the time I have spent with the Royal Shakespeare Company and with companies in other parts of the world, most particularly with Theatre For A New Audience (TFANA) in New York, and also with directors and writers. The focus is on how we speak text, both classical and modern, in today's world. Looking back, what I find so wonderful is that it has all seemed to happen by chance.

I suppose all the work is about freeing the subconscious response of the speaker to the words she or he is speaking, and thus releasing the underlying nuances of meaning through its rhythm and structure – that is its bottom line. The strategies that I will be laying out to achieve this are what I call 'displacement strategies'. It is also about the language being in the body as well as the mind, and this is where the work which has to do with some kind of resistance can release the physical response to the text and open up unexpected possibilities in the language. Most important, we must never forget that this response to language will be different for each person, how we hear it and how we perceive its meaning – and that is as it should be.

Up until the time I joined the Royal Shakespeare Company I had been teaching Voice at the Central School of Speech and Drama in London, mainly working with the acting students. It was a great beginning, for I was working alongside other Voice people, plus

Speech Therapists, so that we were always learning from each other and taking the work forward and we were also learning from that amazing teacher, Gwynneth Thurburn, who ran the school. Thurbie, as she was called, was passionate about poetry, and this suited me as I had a like passion. She was also a very positive presence in one's life, for she taught you never to be satisfied, but she also nurtured and encouraged.

The work was of course very much centred on the technical aspects of the voice which were covered extremely thoroughly – breathing, relaxation, and the muscularity of the lips and tongue – so that each student actor had a good grounding in their own vocal resource. In order to make this work practical, a great deal of time was also given to what were called 'diction' classes – these classes focused on the speaking of prose and verse. It was the verse that interested me particularly, partly because of my own love for it, but also because I perceived its importance in the training of the actors' ear, and their perception of rhythm and cadence in often complex writing (like metaphysical poetry, for instance). This work was given top priority at Central, and the benefit to actors was enormous, for it gave them the opportunity to discover and hear for themselves the infinite variety of cadence and rhythm in one piece of text, be it verse or prose. It is something which takes time to discover, but is what will entrap the ear of the listener. It is very sad, I think, that drama schools today do not prioritise this work in the same way: there is so much focus put on training for film and television – ie, what we look like – and very little on how we are heard. I suppose this reflects our culture at the moment, yet I do believe that the voice can draw people in, simply by its vibration and by the way it can stir our curiosity through that slight lift in the cadence, and make us want to listen.

Over the same period of time I did a great deal of private work with actors, some very experienced and well-known, working on their voices and perhaps helping them with scripts that they were about to undertake, either for theatre or for film. I also ran my own weekly class for actors in a studio in Drury Lane.

When, in 1969, Trevor Nunn invited me to work with the RSC, this was the challenge I needed. Trevor, Terry Hands and John Barton were the three main directors there at the time and, happily for me, each had a very different approach to text. I learnt so much about the dynamics of rhythm and structure from them, thus forcing me to find different approaches to open up the actors' responses to the texts they were working on.

My initial brief was to ensure that the actors, particularly those new to the Company, could fill the Main House – our only auditorium at that time – without strain, yet keep the intimacy, the reality, needed between the characters on stage. But the work soon became more than about vocal projection; it became about how the actor managed the speaking of the text in the space so that it could be heard all over the house, yet keep true to the needs of the scene. Now this sense of intimacy, this truth, was something particularly integral to Trevor Nunn's work. It was at a time when speaking on stage required a more formal approach than we are accustomed to now – although I think we were already at a turning point then. My job was somehow to achieve the naturalism that I perceived Trevor wanted from the actor, with the size the actor needed, both vocal and imaginative, in order to reach the edges of the auditorium. In order to help the actor I would find as big a space as possible in the building (working spaces were always at a premium) and get them to do their scenes very quietly across that space, so that they became aware of the area beyond the stage: for actors always need that double awareness – the space they are playing with on stage, and the space between them and the audience. Speaking quietly across a space in this way made them more aware of the value of the words themselves, so that they could find the size of the language, the imagery, yet keep a sense of people talking quietly together. It is a balance that we constantly have to practise, for that balance is as important now as it was then.

The work with Terry Hands and John Barton needed quite different tactics. With Hands, for instance, intimacy was not an issue, for his work was nearly always of an epic nature requiring pace and a more open approach. Because of his demand for speed, the actor could too easily lose the detail within a speech, and my way of dealing with this was to get the actor to speak the text very quietly, and to make the details very precise, so that in the end they could find the speed that was wanted without losing the different textures in the language. Barton's demands were also very different. He wanted the structure of the text to be clearly honoured – the specifics of rhythm, antithesis, metaphor and word play – and new ways were needed to deal with this. Actors would come to my small upstairs office to go over their speeches; having gone through the necessary voice work in order to release their own private reaction to the language, I would perhaps throw a handful of books on the floor and get them to pick them up and put them in order on the shelf while going through their part. A simple procedure, but I soon realised how, by doing a simple task while speaking, the actor was freed up and so allowed him or her to find their own response to the text, while still honouring the speech structures that Barton wanted, thus keeping the essence of the director's concept and style. This was the beginning: the direct connection with the rehearsal process enabled me to develop the work which had been waiting subconsciously to be put to use. But I was extremely lucky in that I had the full support of those three directors, Nunn, Hands and Barton, who not only took my work on board, but also realised its value to the actors and so gave me time with them.

As the Company expanded I had the opportunity to work with a number of different directors, on new work as well as classical, each with different rehearsal processes, all of which helped me to firm up on my own ways of enabling the actor to fulfil both the requirements of the production and their own potential as an artist. Also at this time my work in schools, youth and community groups, and later in prisons, jogged me into developing ways of working so that people could enter the language, whatever their reading ability or knowledge of literature, without any barriers. I discovered that if you put some resistance in the way of the speaker in order to take their mind off getting the words right and making the sense clear, people actively engaged with the language and made it their own – it allowed the language to take over. Certainly some of the exercises came into being out of desperation to make a group become involved in what they were saying, and so have a deeper understanding of its content.

I have written in detail about all these influences in *Text in Action*. However there is one instance which I would like to repeat because I feel it is such a clear example of how we can be affected by words, and gain a deeper insight through them. A while ago I was doing a series of workshops for the ILEA in London.[1] In this particular workshop I was looking at *Othello* with a group of upper-sixth-form boys. I chose to look at the centre scene – Act Three, Scene Three – where Iago, by his subtle inferences, ignites Othello's jealousy, and it results in that wonderful speech of Othello:

IAGO: Patience, I say: your mind perhaps may change.
OTHELLO: Never, Iago. Like to the Pontic sea,
           Whose icy current and compulsive course
           Ne'er feels retiring ebb, but keeps due on
           To the Propontic and the Hellespont,
           Even so my bloody thoughts with violent pace
           Shall ne'er look back, ne'er ebb to humble love,
           Till that a capable and wide revenge
           Swallow them up. Now, by yond marble heaven,
           In the due reverence of a sacred vow
           I here engage my words.

They were an intelligent group, and of course they all knew what it meant, but as we went through the speech together I knew they were totally unmoved by it, and even uninterested. In my frustration I got them to stand up and link arms in a circle round the room (which was full of desks), and read it through again, but this time pulling against each other as hard as they could – quite difficult when you have a book in your hand. The result was quite chaotic; they fell against each other and desks went over. At first they thought it was funny, but when we repeated the exercise they became involved with the language and started to commit to it in a

---

1   See *Text in Action*, 40–1.

different way: although they knew the exercise was set up they still found it frustrating to be pulled about in this way and not be able to get the words out properly, and this impacted on the language itself, for it became forceful and strong. At the end one young man said, 'I see how he feels – he is drowning in his feelings'. That for me said it all: the group had felt the power of the language and the power of the thoughts somewhere within themselves, and that language and its meaning will always stay with them.

The other very important input into my work has been my association with Theatre For A New Audience in New York, and their Artistic Director Jeffrey Horowitz. I have been working with the actors in the Company on their productions for twelve years, and for the last seven of those years I have also led workshops for directors, which have been extremely well organised. It has worked like this: five or six directors are invited to attend and, before the session starts, each one chooses two scenes that they would like to work on, usually one Shakespeare and one Jacobean or perhaps modern; these scenes are then cast with actors who work for the Company. Over the first few days I do voice and text work with the whole group – actors and directors – and talk through the possible strategies they might use when working; they then split into their groups to work their chosen scenes. While this is happening, I look in on each group and make suggestions with regard to exercises which I think would be useful. At the end of the work period, everyone gathers and each group shows their scene. These workshops have been invaluable for me in that I have been able to test out and develop the strategies I have evolved in a very practical way, and I have been able to assess their value.

But of course my abiding influence has, and always will be, Peter Brook. I was able to be part of his team on the celebrated 1970 production of *A Midsummer Night's Dream*, and it was with him that I realised the importance, or should I say the art, of listening: how the actor listens to the words, to their fellow actors and to the world of the play, and in doing this how the language can fly in unexpected ways. It was Peter who validated my own work and gave me the belief in it which was so necessary in order for it to develop fully. It was a time of revelation for me.

I felt it was important to write all this in order to make quite clear that the work I will be laying out in this book has its roots firmly in the creative rehearsal process, and hopefully will fuse both concept and character development with the structure and sound of the text itself.

As I have already said in Chapter One, every play is a world and every language names a culture: it surely then must follow that in the language of a play we find its world. If we believe this then we have to give the actors time to find that common language together – plus their own character's response to it. If we take time at the beginning of rehearsal to do just that the actor will feel free to trust the language, or as I like to think, live in it and use it imaginatively, so that they can identify with its sound in their own private voice, and not by feeling that they must 'speak it right' and make sense. It is that inner world of the play they need to evoke through the words.

Areas of Work

1 Workshop in Brief

Because I want this book to be practical as quickly as possible, I want to begin in Chapter Three by setting out a workshop which can be done at the beginning of a rehearsal period. It may take people by surprise, but that in itself is a good thing because then there is no time to get nervous. I think it is important to bring out the joy of working on language which is expressive, and which is able to touch something deep within oneself.

2 Group Work on Form and Structure

In Chapter Four I want to look at ways by which we can work on the form and structure of the text of a play, be it classical or modern. We will be looking in detail at the way the language takes us into the world of the play, through its rhythm and thought structures, the texture of the language and the images used. It is so good to do this work as a group for it gets everyone on the same wavelength, listening collectively and talking about the issues, and so dispensing of any misgivings that the individual actor may have. It helps to create the world.

3 Rehearsal Strategies

The heart of this book is Chapter Five, where I set out the various rehearsal strategies which I have developed, and which can be used creatively during the preparation period in order to open up the possibilities of story, character and text. I believe they are a central part of the rehearsal process, for they make us hear the language in an active and often surprising way, plus they uncover the subtext beneath the surface – the world in the language. In other words, they put the spoken text at the centre of the creative process.

I call them 'Displacement Strategies' for, by giving the actor a task or an intention which is not part of the demands of the play, the actor finds a freedom with the text which they would probably not otherwise discover. As I have already said, this strand of work developed from my wish to free the actor and give them the space, just for a moment, to discover their own very personal response to the text unshaped by anything that may have been discussed in rehearsal.

So, all the exercises that I will list in Chapter Five in some way take the conscious mind away from the text that is written down and release a subconscious, subliminal response to it. The work thus releases the imagination of the speaker. I cannot put it more clearly than that – I only know it works. Perhaps it releases the anarchy which is there underneath us all.

4 Collective Work

It is always good for the group to work together on texts other than the play in hand, in order to alert them to their collective response to language. Working on other texts gives the actor a greater freedom to experiment, and working as a group is always enriching because of the variety of response, and because it cannot be judgmental in any way. This work also lays the habit of listening: now

31

I know all actors listen, but so often it is with a pre-conscious ear and not an ear alert to the moment of hearing, and however many times you have played the text it will always be different. We must never be too 'ready', for this will not excite either the other actor or the person who is listening. This forms the first part of Chapter Six.

5 The Space

In Chapter Six we will also be looking at space and how that affects the voice, plus the very necessary work which should be done when you get into the acting area itself, be it a theatre space of whatever size, or a small studio space where it is often difficult to judge the right volume needed, and where the set itself will also have an effect on the voice.

Every space by its very size has a different acoustic, plus so many things affect that acoustic: for instance, if there is a lot of wood or brick around, the sound can become over-bright, and this will affect the voice, making it sound too sharp and thin. Conversely, if the stage is carpeted or if there is a lot of hanging material or plastic substance in the set, this will soak up the sound and muffle it, and the actor may need to use a slightly higher tone to compensate for this, for a low voice can lose its edge and get lost. It is crucial that actors are given time to experience and play around with the acoustic for themselves, so that they can make the necessary adjustments of volume and pitch and so feel comfortable and confident wherever they are within that space. If there is difficulty in being heard it is seldom to do with volume, but much more to do with the pitch and muscularity of the speaking. (Perhaps directors and designers should also look into these issues more deeply when designing for the space being used.)

6 The Voice Itself

As a prelude to the work on text, we do need to establish work on the voice itself – I like to call it 'sitting down in the voice', and it is covered in Chapter Seven. It is essential that the actor continues to focus on finding that sound from their centre, for it gives the voice a certain authority, a 'thisness', that draws in the audience. The more experienced the actor, the more skilful the use of the voice:

yet there is ever a consciousness there, an underlying need to reach over to the audience as evocatively as possible, and this will always make for that slight physical tension in the upper part of the body, and then the true vibration of the voice is lost.

I believe that there is a great benefit in starting off rehearsals with a good Voice session: I think we each have some underlying doubt about how we sound to other people, and simply to have the freedom to experiment with each other is both releasing and enriching. Of course as you get further into the rehearsal period time will get limited, but I believe it is important to keep this work going even if in much shorter stints, and you will be surprised how much enjoyment and freedom the group will get out of it. If you have a Voice person with you, that of course would be the best, however if you are not lucky enough to have one then I go on to lay out a full voice session which you can initially work through, and subsequently use parts of it. As time gets limited, actors should be encouraged to do their own warm-up sessions before rehearsal, and most certainly before each performance.

I would say here that this is a structure that I use not only with the Royal Shakespeare Company when embarking on a new rehearsal period, but also with other theatre companies both in the UK and abroad – also in other languages. I would also use the same format with community groups, schools or in a prison. These groups do not necessarily find the same artistic relevance as the actor, but they do most certainly find the sense of the language through its very sound and rhythm, and so hopefully get a different and richer understanding from it. The work opens up new perceptions of language that we understand through the sound of words as well as their literal meaning, and this makes them feel that the text is not exclusive to those with learning but belongs equally to every-one, and this gives them the impetus to explore the written text with a greater freedom.

SECTION TWO
The Work Itself

Chapter Three

INTRODUCTORY WORKSHOP

PART OF ME wants to call this a 'whirlwind workshop' because in its essence it covers a number of the areas that I have already listed, and it does so very quickly. Why I feel this is good is that by covering so much in such a short time it will not only surprise the group you are working with, but it will also make them aware of the incredible variety of energies – rhythms and movements of thought – which can be found in any given text, but which you cannot necessarily pin down. By getting the group to feel this in their bodies it will hopefully make them alert to the delight and spontaneity in the language, which we will then go on to work at in detail. The point of this is that we should never lose that delight in the verbalising of ideas precisely expressed. But perhaps the most important thing about it is that by working with speed on texts that are not necessarily familiar to the group, it takes away any inhibitions about doing it 'right': because they do not know the text, they are not weighed down with preconceptions, or a feeling they must do it well, and consequently they are more open to the possibilities.

In a fairly swift and unpressured way the workshop alerts the ear to the possibilities of sound and rhythm and cadence. It will also make us aware of our own sound and how we can feel it in our bodies and, as I have said, by doing the work together it takes the pressure off the individual to do it 'right'. I never feel that I am teaching anybody, I am simply alerting them to the language and its music, and giving them the 'let' to find their own response. That response will be, and I stress *should* be, different for each person: it is totally non-judgemental. It also prepares us for the detailed work ahead.

The focus is on Shakespeare – partly, of course, because his works are my priority, be it in this country or abroad, but it is chiefly because there is so much freedom and variety in the language, plus a dynamic in the rhythm and sound, that it quickens the reflexes of the speaker and gives the actor a great freedom of response. Shakespeare somehow wrote the spoken word in all its glorious variability – roughness, humour, tenderness. However, the exercises themselves work for all texts, both classical and modern.

As I have said, it is simply a working structure, and once you have tried it out you will see what is useful, and what perhaps you would like to change. I believe the progression of exercises will make the actors aware of the issues to look out for, hopefully in a very practical way, and I hope will demystify areas which may have seemed difficult.

However if, because of time, it is not possible to do the whole workshop in one go, or if it does not seem quite appropriate, then take it through in two or three different parts. The important thing is that the actors get the language off the page and into their bodies, and at the same time get a sense that the structure of the language, the shaping of a speech, is not some academic rule that has to be obeyed, but is part and parcel of its meaning and can be enjoyed as such.

It is best in this initial workshop to use texts other than the text you will be working on, but of course as you get into rehearsal these same exercises can be used to specific ends, as we shall see. Set aside two hours if possible for this first session because it will take time for the group to enter the work and realise its potential, but any further group work can of course be much shorter, and will in any case be related to the work in progress. Also, because out of necessity they will be reading the text for the first time, it will take longer for them to grasp the language and the meaning fully. But I need to stress one thing – it is extremely important right at the beginning to ascertain if there are any dyslexics in the group: because of their different spatial awareness they may need a little more time to get around the words on the page, but if you give them a little space they will be fine. The group will of course have very varying degrees of acting experience behind them, but embrace this for it can be very enriching. I do think there is a value in covering a spread of work in this way so that we can open up to the diversity of the language and get pleasure from it.

Preparation

The first ten minutes should be given over to the actors for their own vocal preparation so that they feel in touch with their own voice and their own centre. If you have a voice person with you they will of course lead the work, but I have put an outline for a short vocal warm-up in Chapter Seven (pages 161–4).

Now for the text...

Metre and Movement of Thought

I like to start by getting everyone moving so they cannot think too much – surprise is always a good ploy. So first we will look at Sonnet 129 –

> Th'expense of spirit in a waste of shame
> Is lust in action; and till action, lust
> Is perjur'd, murderous, bloody, full of blame,
> Savage, extreme, rude, cruel, not to trust;
> Enjoy'd no sooner but despisèd straight;
> Past reason hunted; and no sooner had,
> Past reason hated, as a swallow'd bait
> On purpose laid to make the taker mad, –
> Mad in pursuit, and in possession so;
> Had, having, and in quest to have, extreme;
> A bliss in proof; and prov'd, a very woe;
> Before, a joy propos'd; behind, a dream.
> > All this the world well knows; yet none knows well
> > To shun the heav'n that leads men to this hell.

38

- First get the group to gently read it through together – it is important not to rush this as people read at different speeds.
- They then should walk round the space reading it for themselves in their own time so they have both the time and space to discover their own response. If you think it necessary let them do this twice.
- Then gather them together in order to talk over its meaning.
- They will obviously have realised it is about sex and lust: however this is where you do need to clarify that the word 'spirit' is a euphemism for semen – there can then be no doubt about the central theme.
- When they have had time to get hold of the meaning for themselves, get them to speak it quite firmly, being aware of the muscularity of the language, while briskly walking round the space.
- Repeat this but this time ask them to change direction on every punctuation mark.
- You will have to let them do this a couple of times, as moving and speaking quite fast at the same time can be confusing: the important thing is to make sure they really change direction on the marks quite sharply.
- Now get them to stand in a group, quite close, and speak it again – this time jostling each other as they speak.

It is time now to find out what they have gleaned.

- By changing direction on the punctuation marks in this way they will have become aware of how the thoughts are constantly on the move – one thought springing out of the next.
- In this sonnet the constant movement of the thoughts puts the speaker in touch with the restlessness and angry passion in the writing.
- The jostling together will make each person unconsciously find the muscularity and force of the language, for although the group knows that the jostling has been set up as an exercise, it

is still very irritating to be pushed about in this way, and this will provoke them quite subconsciously into expressing that irritation in their speech – this will result in the extra muscularity of the consonants.

- It is really important that they recognise this muscularity as not being forced or false.

So much can be learned from all this.

- How the movement of thoughts, be they quick or slow, is integral to how the character thinks, and so tells us much about the state of mind of that character.

- And because the movement involves the whole body the language is connected with our whole self and not just the mind.

- Also by finding the muscularity of the consonants and how they embody the thoughts, we become aware of those thoughts as actions provoking new thoughts.

The next thing we need to discover, or I should rather say 'to hear', is the basic metre and how that interacts with the movement of the thoughts. So we need to beat out the metre and find how it works in conjunction with the sense, and also with the length of the words themselves.

We will find that it is fairly regular, though some lines are rather full and have to be negotiated. But we will also hear when it breaks quite radically and how that affects the meaning and its underlying inferences – the subtext in other words. By 'negotiated' I mean that, although each line is of a constant length, some phrases can be spoken quite quickly in order to give space to the longer phrases; plus the length of a phrase is also dependent on the varying lengths of the vowels and consonants within it. As Peter Brook would say – 'There are a million ways of saying one line': that to me is a fundamental truth.

I think the best and clearest way forward is to speak the whole sonnet through, tapping out the metre as you go, noticing how the metre and sense stress interact. You will then get an idea of the sound of the sonnet as a whole.

So, it is written in iambic pentameter – ie, five strong beats and ten syllables – thus –

te-tum te-tum te-tum te-tum te-tum

plus there is always the possibility of that break, or poise, in the middle of a line – the caesura – to allow the critical word to land. Now as we go through it in more detail we will make the points regarding metre, stress, vowel and consonant lengths etc. which need to be served. How you use these will vary from person to person, and will be determined by each speaker's response to the language plus their individual perception of the basic meaning or purpose underlying these fourteen lines: the timing therefore will always be variable. The important thing is to hear how the words are continually in play with the stress.

We will take the first four lines separately: in these lines the metre stress is marked as follows –

Th' expense of spirit in a waste of shame
Is lust in action: and till action, lust
Is perjured, murderous, bloody, full of blame,
Savage, extreme, rude, cruel, not to trust...

Line 1

- The syllables in the first half of the line are short, short vowels and unvoiced consonants.

- This gives space for the caesura, or slight break, after 'spirit', in order to let that word, with its *double entendre*, land on the ear of the listener.

- It then gives room for the slightly longer vowels in 'waste of shame', and the emotional implications of those words.

- The last half of the line then takes longer to speak than the first half.

Line 2

- This is also fairly regular.
- The word 'lust' needs a moment for its full meaning to land.
- Again we need that slight break after 'in action', the caesura, to allow the whole thought to drop in.
- But we make up for that time on the last half of the line – yet allowing that the word 'lust' has to lift at the end in order to let us hear the whole thought through into the next line.
- It also gives the poet time to find the words to describe it – quite extreme words; and we have to be made ready for them.

Line 3

- This line is interesting because the words are much fuller in sound, the long 'er' sounds and the voiced consonants.
- Then 'bloody' which knocks the rhythm about.
- Then the relatively short 'full of' so that you can lay the weight on 'blame': you immediately hear the syncopation in the lines.

Line 4

- This is wonderful because the rhythm is totally broken by that first word 'savage' – it breaks the metre immediately, for there is no way you can make it fit in – and so the word of itself becomes savage and brutal: at once we know where the sonnet is grounded.
- Then the syncopation of the subsequent 'rude, cruel not to trust' – ie, the long 'oo' sounds followed by the short 'not to trust'.

The next four lines are fairly regular in rhythm, but the images are cruel and need to be given time to drop in:

> Enjoyéd no sooner but despiséd straight,
> Past reason hunted, and no sooner had
> Past reason hated, as a swallowed bait
> On purpose laid to make the taker mad.

The first three lines have that slight break in the middle in order to clarify the thought, and to point up the antitheses of 'enjoyed' and 'despised' and 'sooner' and 'straight', or 'hunted' and 'hated' on the following two lines – they are vicious-sounding words. That word 'bait', with its implicit cruelty, has to be allowed to land, for it leads us to the unbroken relentlessness of 'On purpose laid to make the taker mad' – no break there, plus the repetition of the vowels in 'laid' and 'taker', and the length of the word 'mad' point this up.

The next four lines are relatively straightforward in their measure:

> Mad in pursuit and in possession so,
> Had, having, and in quest to have, extreme;
> A bliss in proof, and proved a very woe;
> Before, a joy proposed; behind, a dream.

- The first line breaks on the first word 'mad', but the rest is quite smooth.
- In the second line the metre is broken on the first two words 'Had, having...', but it again rights itself in the last half of the line.
- The vowel sounds are quite long, eg 'extreme', 'woe', 'proposed', 'dream'.

This brings us, by its more even sound, towards a conclusion – to the weight of the final couplet which cannot be hurried:

> All this the world well knows, yet none knows well
> To shun the heav'n that leads men to this hell.

All is summed up in these two lines which is given its weight by those long vowel sounds and continuant consonants – 'all', 'world', 'knows', 'well', 'hell', etc. Nor can you hurry the wonderful existential irony they contain: so much movement, so many thoughts.

That Other World

Our next quest is for that 'other world' – the world into which we are taken by the actor – the words themselves take us there. I want to do this by looking at the beginnings of two plays – *Hamlet* and *A Midsummer Night's Dream.*

Hamlet (I i): The group should first sit on the floor in a circle and read this first scene down to line 52.

BARNARDO: Who's there?

FRANCISCO: Nay, answer me, Stand and unfold yourself.

BARNARDO: Long live the King!

FRANCISCO: Barnardo?

BARNARDO: He.

FRANCISCO: You come most carefully upon your hour.

BARNARDO: 'Tis now struck twelve. Get thee to bed, Francisco.

FRANCISCO: For this relief much thanks. 'Tis bitter cold,
And I am sick at heart.

BARNARDO: Have you had quiet guard?

FRANCISCO: Not a mouse stirring.

BARNARDO: Well, good night.
If you do meet Horatio and Marcellus,
The rivals of my watch, bid them make haste.

Enter HORATIO and MARCELLUS.

FRANCISCO: I think I hear them. Stand ho! Who is there?

HORATIO: Friends to this ground.

MARCELLUS: And liegemen to the Dane.

FRANCISCO: Give you good night.

MARCELLUS: O, farewell, honest soldier,
Who hath relieved you?

FRANCISCO: Barnardo hath my place.
Give you good night.

Exit.

MARCELLUS: Holla Barnardo!

BARNARDO: Say –

	What, is Horatio there?
HORATIO:	A piece of him.
BARNARDO:	Welcome, Horatio. Welcome, good Marcellus.,
MARCELLUS:	What, has this thing appeared again tonight?
BARNARDO:	I have seen nothing.

Horatio says 'tis but our fantasy,
And will not let belief take hold of him
Touching this dreaded sight twice seen of us.
Therefore I have entreated him along
With us to watch the minutes of this night,
That, if again this apparition come,
He may approve our eyes and speak to it.

HORATIO: Tush, tush, 'twill not appear.

BARNARDO: Sit down awhile,
And let us once again assail your ears,
That are so fortified against our story,
What we have two nights seen.

HORATIO: Well, sit we down,
And let us hear Barnardo speak of this.

BARNARDO: Last night of all,
When yond same star that's westward from the pole
Had made his course t'illume that part of heaven
Where now it burns, Marcellus and myself,
The bell then beating one –

Enter the GHOST.

MARCELLUS: Peace, break thee off. Look where it comes again.
BARNARDO: In the same figure like the King that's dead.
MARCELLUS: Thou art a scholar. Speak to it, Horatio.
BARNARDO: Looks 'a not like the King? Mark it, Horatio.
HORATIO: Most like. It harrows me with fear and wonder.
BARNARDO: It would be spoke to.
MARCELLUS: Speak to it, Horatio.
HORATIO: What art thou that usurpest this time of night,
Together with that fair and warlike form
In which the majesty of buried Denmark

> Did sometimes march? By heaven I charge thee, speak.
> MARCELLUS: It is offended.
> BARNARDO: See, it stalks away.
> HORATIO: Stay, speak. I charge thee, speak.
>
> *Exit the GHOST.*
>
> MARCELLUS: 'Tis gone and will not answer.

- Let the group read it round in the circle each taking a speech, or part of a speech, depending on its length. Do this a couple of times so they feel easy reading it.

- Now choose four actors and allot them each a character; these four should then move into the middle and read the scene again. It is important that the others in the group should not look at the script – they should simply listen.

- As they listen, ask them to mutter the words they hear which refer to 'the other' – by that I mean words which have a reference to something which is not quite tangible, not solid.

- They will perhaps repeat – 'this thing' – 'it' – 'fantasy' – 'apparition', etc, also they will notice those enigmatic answers, for example – 'Not a mouse stirring', and 'A piece of him' – which bring an odd and chilling atmosphere to the place.

- Now let these four actors go to the four different corners of the space, with the rest of the group standing in the middle – or they can move quietly around.

- Ask the actors to read the scene again, this time speaking as quietly as possible, yet reaching across to the character opposite – let it be almost a whisper. By reaching across quietly in this way they will probably slightly extend the words so that the length and texture of those sounds will be more apparent. (Right at the beginning, for instance: 'Who's there' – the length of that first vowel as it reaches across the space is particularly evocative.)

46

- The group should continue to mutter very quietly the words that sit with them through the scene: they will hear the sense of foreboding in the language, and the questions – but there are no direct answers.

What is also very telling is the rhythm. If we take it as written in strict five-beat iambic lines (which I personally do), we will notice the spaces:

Line 1
'Who's there?' – two words only but taking the space of one line.

Line 2
This line is one complete iambic pentameter.

Line 3
'Long live the king' – two iambic beats:) these three lines may

Line 4
'Barnardo.' – one word only:) be spoken as one
) four-beat line – but it

Line 5
'He.' – again one word only:) still makes spaces.

)

)

)

)

)

)

Line 6
'You come most carefully upon your hour.' – one full iambic line.

Line 7
''Tis now struck twelve. Get thee to bed, Francisco.' – regular iambic line.

Lines 8–9
'For this relief much thanks. 'Tis bitter cold,
And I am sick at heart.'
– half line only, so there is a space.

Lines 10–11
'Have you had quiet guard?'/'Not a mouse stirring.' – one complete line.

Lines 12–14
'Well, good night.
If you do meet Horatio and Marcellus,
The rivals of my watch, bid them make haste.'
– and so on through this first section of the scene.

Now of course if we were to read this scene to ourselves we would be able to work out its literal meaning quite easily, for it is quite straightforward. We would notice that it was written in iambic metre, some lines being broken and we would 'appreciate' the slightly off-beat images and the references to the ghost. But if we read it through aloud hearing those spaces and hearing those slightly ambiguous references we are drawn into this other world; we become aware of this sense of otherness, of not knowing what is going to happen, this feeling of disquiet, which is at the heart of the play. It has an extraordinary music throughout, which comes to an end when Marcellus says –

'Tis gone and will not answer.

Yet throughout the scene the soldiers are being as sensible as possible.

The next part of the scene has a much steadier sound, Horatio and the soldiers are being practical and the rhythm is regular – until of course the Ghost returns.

But it is those first two words – 'Who's there?' – that surely are the centre line of the play, the question that the play is trying to answer, and Hamlet also. Now if those first two words are swallowed up in soldiers' business and a barking soldierly sound, and therefore negated – as so often happens – then that centre goes unnoticed. So how does the actor, the soldier, lay those first two words on the audience, without any seeming stress, yet feeding our subconscious ear?

Always feel free to take the exercises in different directions; for instance, you may like to get some of the group to stand behind the actors who are speaking and whisper the words in their ear as they are spoken. The important thing is that we heighten our awareness of the words and where they take us, so that we can make the words drop into the audience's awareness without undue emphasis. It is nearly always in the timing – those moments between words.

I would also like to stress again how important it is when starting this text work that you find out whether there is anyone dyslexic in the group, for they may feel at a disadvantage. There is of course no problem, they just need to feel they can take their own time and be comfortable with it.

Now for the world of the *Dream*. To begin with, we will look at these first three speeches of Theseus and Hippolyta and hear where they take us:

THESEUS: Now, fair Hippolyta, our nuptial hour
Draws on apace. Four happy days bring in
Another moon – but O, methinks how slow
This old moon wanes! She lingers my desires,
Like to a step dame or a dowager
Long withering out a young man's revenue.

HIPPOLYTA: Four days will quickly steep themselves in night;
Four nights will quickly dream away the time:
And then the moon – like to a silver bow
New-bent in heaven – shall behold the night
Of our solemnities.

THESEUS: Go, Philostrate,
Stir up the Athenian youth to merriments.
Awake the pert and nimble spirit of mirth.
Turn melancholy forth to funerals:
The pale companion is not for our pomp.

Exit PHILOSTRATE.

Hippolyta, I wooed thee with my sword,
And won thy love doing thee injuries;
But I will wed thee in another key:
With pomp, with triumph, and with revelling.[1]

---

1 *A Midsummer Night's Dream*, I i.

- First get the whole group to walk round in the space, speaking the text quite quietly for themselves.

- It helps for them to speak it a couple of times through on their own for then they start to notice things in the text for themselves – plus if they are walking about they are not aware of how anyone else is speaking it, which can not only be inhibiting but can also distract from their own response to the language.

Having read those first three speeches together, ask two actors to read the parts of Theseus and Hippolyta.

- To do this they should stand opposite each other in the space with a little distance between them, and speak the lines through.

- When they are comfortable with this, get them to move further away from each other, with the rest of the group standing around.

- As they speak it through again ask the group to mutter the words which have any sexual connotation as they hear them. This will no doubt surprise, for so many of the words have just that touch of sensuality – 'lingers', 'withering', 'moon', 'silver bow', 'stir up the Athenian youth', etc, which together create a strong sexual ambience. But, of course, the real sexuality comes with Theseus' words:

> Hippolyta, I wooed thee with my sword...

- And suddenly we realise this is not going to be a comfortable journey, but that we are going to be taken into quite a dark place.

Now let us take this a step further and explore the physical nature of the language and how, by involving the whole body in the speaking, the actor may find another layer of meaning – and of passion.

- So, again get the two actors to stand opposite each other, quite a distance apart. Then ask two of the group to stand behind Theseus, and two behind Hippolyta.

- As the two actors speak the text their intention must be to get to each other, but as they do so the actors behind them must try to prevent this and keep them apart.

- This is a simple (and perhaps rather crude) exercise, but you will hear how the physical need of the actors to get to each other will make the language come from a deeper place in their bodies – we will hear that physicality in their voices.

- We will also hear how that need to reach out will extend the length of the vowels as they speak, and so prove that language can be extended by extreme feeling and desire without being emotionally 'over the top'.

This is very important both to experience and to trust because, as with all text both classical and modern, we need to find that happy point between extravagance and 'cool' which can express the size of the character's feelings. When doing the exercise it is important that the actors keeping them apart do not get too rough, or the meaning and intention will be overshadowed.

Neither of these exercises are difficult, but they help us to pinpoint two areas of work:

1 Just how much the word takes us into the world, the whole ethos of the play. Plus just how much the actor has to lay that world through words without stressing them or signalling them in any way: 'Who's there' would not take us into any other play but *Hamlet*.

2 Language can be extreme when the need is there, for it costs. When the actor is working in depth on a part, to put some form of difficulty or resistance in their path will often help them release the emotion into the language. We will be looking into this in many different ways as we go.

Movement of Thought Into Character

Now I want to take the work we did on Sonnet 129 (page 38), into character, and to look at how the thoughts move, how one thought kicks off the next and builds through a speech, so that we get the impression that the character has not decided what the end will be until they get there – but by the very words they choose that end is inevitable.

We will take a very straightforward example, the speech of Egeus in the *Dream*, almost immediately after the opening speeches of Theseus and Hippolyta.

EGEUS: Full of vexation come I, with complaint
               Against my child, my daughter Hermia.
               Stand forth, Demetrius! My noble lord,
               This man hath my consent to marry her.
               Stand forth, Lysander! – And, my gracious Duke,
               This man hath bewitched the bosom of my child.
               Thou, thou, Lysander, thou hast given her rhymes,
               And interchanged love-tokens with my child.
               Thou hast by moonlight at her window sung
               With feigning voice verses of feigning love,
               And stolen the impression of her fantasy.
               With bracelets of thy hair, rings, gauds, conceits,
               Knacks, trifles, nosegays, sweetmeats – messengers
               Of strong prevailment in unhardened youth –
               With cunning hast thou filched my daughter's heart,
               Turned her obedience which is due to me
               To stubborn harshness. And, my gracious Duke,
               Be it so she will not here before your grace
               Consent to marry with Demetrius,
               I beg the ancient privilege of Athens:
               As she is mine, I may dispose of her;
               Which shall be either to this gentleman
               Or to her death, according to our law
               Immediately provided in that case.[1]

- First let the group read it through walking briskly round in the space.

---

1 *A Midsummer Night's Dream*, I i.

- Do this again, but this time have them change directions on each punctuation mark (as for Sonnet 129) – it should be brisk and sharp and maybe they should beat through a few of the lines just to get a feel of its texture.

- Then gather all together and talk through anything that they may have found difficult.

Now get one person to take the part of Egeus and read it through so that the group can listen objectively.

- Next, in order to highlight Egeus' thought processes, place two chairs next to each other in the centre of the space, and ask the actor reading Egeus to start by sitting on one chair.

- At every punctuation mark he should move to the other chair – but he must not speak while he is moving.

- This will seem laborious at first, but soon the reason will become clear, for we will hear in the rhythm how at the beginning Egeus is trying to be reasonable and reasoned, but as he gets going the words he uses become more emotive and the thoughts start to tumble out. Yet he has to keep a semblance of control which he does by every so often breaking his flow to say 'My gracious Duke' or 'My noble lord'.

- As the actor goes through the speech, the group should mutter words that drop into their consciousness. They will surely repeat the word 'bewitch'd', which to me is at the centre of his thoughts, for the word carries with it a belief in witchcraft, which again opens the dark areas of the play.

- As the group repeat words that impact on them, they will notice how the language starts with fairly innocent words such as
'knacks, nosegays'
and then progresses to
'strong prevailments in unhardened youth'
and then
'with cunning hast thou filch'd my daughter's heart'

That word 'filch'd' always carries a very unpleasant inference with it, both by its sound and its very sense of furtiveness: each image springs off the last one and becomes more charged, and this gives him the courage finally to ask the Duke –

> I beg the ancient privilege of Athens:
> As she is mine, I may dispose of her;
> Which shall be either to this gentleman
> Or to her death, according to our law
> Immediately provided in that case.

To us nowadays that is an unthinkable request, and we are taken into very dark territory. But what I think is interesting, and something which to me is at the centre of any speech where the character is working through his or her feelings in search of an answer, is this question – does Egeus know from the beginning that he is going to ask for her death, or is it something he comes to as he finds the words to express his thoughts? How much do the words act on him, and is it by expressing them that he finds his true intent?

This exercise on two chairs throws up so very clearly how one thought triggers the next, and often highlights the absurdities in the argument – and there is always absurdity in Shakespeare.

Now ask someone to read the Duke so that Egeus can to try to make him hear his case:

- Let the Duke walk around in the space with the rest of the group walking around him.

- As Egeus tries to get him to listen the group should get in the way and make it difficult for Egeus to get to him, not by holding him back but just by getting in the way.

- This will give Egeus a task, to get to the Duke, and so will take his conscious mind off the text and allow his subconscious response to come into play: the words will become active in a different way.

- Always resistance, in one form or another, has its effect, for it compounds the need to speak so that the thoughts are ever active – they also cost.

I need to say something here about punctuation. Obviously, the punctuation differs in the different editions of Shakespeare, but whatever edition you are using it is a good guide to the syntax of the thought, and is always helpful. In the end, how you break the thoughts up is a matter of choice for the actor.

Language Textures / Release of Emotion

Now for something quite different – listening for the textures and emotions filling the language. The texture of the language – ie, the fullness or sharpness of both vowels and consonants – is always integral to the emotional drive of the character. The vowels can be either long or short; the consonants can be sharp explosives or long continuants, of which there may be more than one.

> If it were done when 'tis done, then 'twere well
> It were done quickly…[1]

or –

> What studied torments, tyrant, has for me?[2]

or –

> If there were reason for these miseries
> Then into limits would I bind my woes.[3]

Speaking them out loud you immediately hear how they differ in the length of time they take to speak.

So, first a speech from *Coriolanus*. A speech of Junius Brutus,[4] one of the Tribunes of the people, in conversation with his fellow

---

1 *Macbeth*, I vii.
2 *The Winter's Tale*, III ii. (See page 67).
3 *Titus Andronicus*, III i. (See page 91).
4 Not to be confused with the more famous Brutus in *Julius Caesar*.

Tribune, Sicinius. Coriolanus has gone to the Capitol to seek the voice of the people and it is thought he will be made Consul. Both Brutus and Sicinius are outraged, as they know Coriolanus despises the people; however, at the same time we realise that they too have little respect for the people either – so there is, as so often in Shakespeare, an underlying irony. But the bottom line is this: they do not want Coriolanus to be honoured in this way.

BRUTUS: All tongues speak of him and the blearèd sights
Are spectacled to see him. Your prattling nurse
Into a rapture lets her baby cry
While she chats him. The kitchen malkin pins
Her richest lockram 'bout her reechy neck,
Clambering the walls to eye him. Stalls, bulks, windows
Are smothered up, leads filled, and ridges horsed
With variable complexions, all agreeing
In earnestness to see him. Seld-shown flamens
Do press among the popular throngs and puff
To win a vulgar station. Our veiled dames
Commit the war of white and damask in
Their nicely gawded cheeks to th'wanton spoil
Of Phoebus' burning kisses. Such a pother
As if that whatsoever god who leads him
Were slily crept into his human powers
And gave him graceful posture.[1]

- They will first need to speak it through together a couple of times; it is full of complex images which may take a little time to unravel. But the unfamiliar words are somehow clarified by their sound. For instance:
'kitchen malkin' – a slatternly kitchen maid
'seld-shown flamens' – priests seldom seen in public
'reechy' – dirty, grimy, possibly scraggy

Our imagination takes us there.

---

1 *Coriolanus*, II i.

- When you feel they are ready, get them to speak it very firmly while walking quite briskly round the space, feeling the muscularity of the text.

There are several exercises you can use to find this very pronounced muscularity.

- Ask them to find an object to kick – maybe a small bag, maybe they can take off one of their shoes – and while walking round kick this object on words that grab them: this way they will feel the particular and very male physicality in the language.
- Next, in a close group get them to slightly jostle each other while speaking, making sure that every consonant and every vowel is given its full value: although they know this is set up as an exercise, the actual act of jostling affects how one speaks – it is irritating to be pushed, after all.
- Now get them to speak it through with only one person speaking at a time: anyone can interrupt at any moment – but they must put their hand up as they speak: it may turn out a bit chaotic, but it will stop the language being literal and 'well-behaved, and they will hear that sense of anarchy which is in the character and in language, and which is central to Brutus' frustration.
- You should now go through it again, quite consciously noticing the lengths of the vowels and the fullness of the compound consonants – so often difficult to get one's tongue round. Do not rush this as it is important to experience all the sounds fully – such as:
'all tongues' – 'bleared sights'
'spectacled' – 'prattling nurse'
'kitchen malkin' – 'reechy neck'
'stalls, bulks, windows'
'leads filled and ridges horsed'
'variable complexions'
'seld-shown flamens' – 'popular throngs'
'nicely gawded cheeks'

- What is wonderful is to experience how his very choice of words are difficult to get one's mouth round, and how this difficulty in turn feeds the frustration which he is expressing in the language.

We should now look at the structure – it will tell us more.

- First, you should beat out the metre in order to hear how the metre stress and sense stress knock against each other – they either coincide or have to be negotiated. It is actually fairly regular – there is no violent break as in Sonnet 129 (page 38) – but because the language is so full there is a lot of room for play.

Line 1
This first line has to be negotiated for the first two words – 'All tongues' need equal value. We need that moment of caesura after 'him' to let that premise drop in – him being the subject, the centre, of the speech. Then we have two short words which let us give the length to 'bleared sights'.

Line 2
This is fairly regular – explosive consonants with short vowels, again with the caesura to point up 'him'. Also there is one extra syllable in the middle which has to be negotiated, and which gives a sense of him falling over his words: the end word 'nurse' has to be lifted as it is the subject of the next line.

Line 3
This is regular, the thought carrying through into the next.

Line 4
This is also regular, with the break in the middle again pointing up that word 'him'.

Line 5
Again regular, alliteration on 'richest' and 'reechy' being very evocative in sound: we cannot help but react to that word 'reechy'.

Line 6

A very full line: the stress on the first word reversing the metre; 'clambering' with its extra syllable; long continuant sounds – 'walls', 'stalls', 'bulks' – to be fitted in.

Line 7

Again regular with long, compound consonants – 'leads filled', 'ridges horsed'.

Line 8

Again regular, but with a wonderful movement of vowels – 'variable', 'all agreeing'.

Line 9

A regular line: the caesura in the middle brings to an end a long thought, and it has to be lifted into the next one with the new image – 'seld-shown flamens'.

Line 10

This is again regular, with that ridiculous word 'puff', so evocative, to lift us into the next line. Presumably 'puff' means that their self-importance gains them a seat in the crowd.

Line 11

A regular line, with the caesura in the middle leading us to the next thought, and 'our veiled dames' taking a moment to lay the picture.

Line 12

Again regular – his irony and contempt continue into the next line.

Line 13

Again regular, but his images become increasingly ironic and extravagant leading him into –

Line 14

'Phoebus' burning kisses' – and this takes a moment to lay: the caesura here is important for it makes us wait for that moment when he sums it all up – 'Such a pother...' perhaps he takes a moment to find that word 'pother', for it is both unexpected and ridiculous, and it is the absurdity of that word which expresses both his frustration and his lack of power.

Lines 15–17
The last three lines are regular calm and thoughtful – and almost poetic.

Finally, let us look at its overall shape. As in the late plays, the thoughts are so often complex they carry over into the next line or lines; however, because the thoughts very often end mid-line, at the caesura, the speaker has to mark the end of the thought whilst keeping the rhythm of the whole line intact – quite an art. This means that we need that 'poise' to mark the end of the thought, yet that thought has to project us quickly into the next thought, and this makes a very interesting movement – a kind of restlessness, a need to carry on: it also makes for great variety within the lines themselves. If we do it once through fairly swiftly beating out the metre, we will really feel the the anger in the language.

So, to repeat Brook's words – there are a million ways of saying one line.

To hear this clearly let us do one more exercise with it.

- Divide the group into two – group A and group B.
- Group A starts off by speaking the first sentence/thought down to – 'see him'.
- Group B then takes it on to 'chats him'.
- Group A then takes it down to 'eye him' (a very long thought).
- Group B then goes to 'see him' (even longer).
- And so on to the end of the speech.

It becomes wonderfully apparent how one thought kicks off the next: he cannot wait to get the next thought out, yet at the same time he is enjoying finding the words that express his disgust. In the end we hear Brutus' utter frustration and disgust through the very language he uses and the difficulty he has in uttering it.

- You might want to do this last exercise with just two actors, with the rest of the group listening, and perhaps repeating words that they pick up.

It is a great piece of text to use because, in a very practical way, we can hear just how much the word lengths and the muscularity carry and transmit the underlying mindset of the character. As with the earlier exercise with Egeus (page 52) we become very aware of how the thoughts are continually on the move and self-feeding.

Now to a very different sound and texture. In this soliloquy of Ophelia after she has had a harrowing encounter with Hamlet when he pretends to be mad and refutes any claims regarding her belief in their friendship: she is devastated.

OPHELIA: O, what a noble mind is here o'erthrown!
The courtier's, soldier's, scholar's, eye, tongue, sword,
Th'expectancy and rose of the fair state,
The glass of fashion and the mould of form,
Th'observed of all observers, quite, quite down!
And I, of ladies most deject and wretched,
That suck'd the honey of his music vows,
Now see that noble and most sovereign reason
Like sweet bells jangled, out of time and harsh,
That unmatched form and feature of blown youth
Blasted with ecstasy. O, woe is me
T'have seen what I have seen, see what I see![1]

- First, read it through quite gently together, and talk through any words or images that may need to be clarified.
- Then let the group read it again for themselves, in their own time, walking about the space – they are then not aware of how the others are speaking.
- When you feel they are ready, gather them together and read it through.

---

1 *Hamlet,* III i.

Now for something a little tricky – I want us to experience the vowel sounds on their own, and hear their impact and how they inform the underlying message.

- So, we need to speak the whole speech through but verbalising only the vowel sounds. It will be tricky at first but it will soon become apparent how the vowels can take the meaning through – they may need conducting through it at first, but we will hear those wonderful open vowels in that first line –
  'O, what a noble mind is here overthrown…' – OH – OH – I –
  OH – OH (Oh…noble…mind…overthrown)
  'glass of fashion' – 'mould of form'
  'Th'observed of all observers, quite, quite down!'
  'Now see that noble and most sovereign reason'
  'sweet bells jangled'
  'feature of blown youth'

- To cap it all, the final keening sounds of the last line and a half –
  'O, woe is me
  T'have seen what I have seen, see what I see!'

- They will find this tricky at first, and they must be careful not to make the short sounds glottal or harsh in any way, but the pay-off is in that last line and a half when they will hear how her pain informs the sound, and how the sound informs her pain.

Now for metre stress versus sense stress and how that impacts on the speech as a whole:

Line 1

This is regular, except for that first 'O' which has to be negotiated with 'what'. For that word 'what' carries an underlying meaning of 'to what extent'. Otherwise the important words –'noble' mind' 'here', 'overthrown' carry the stress.

Line 2

Again a regular line, though the end has to be negotiated – 'eye, tongue, sword' – for somehow they have to get equal weight without holding up the rhythm.

Line 3

This again is regular with a little spread on 'rose'.

Line 4

Regular again with those words 'glass' 'fashion', 'mould'. 'form' spreading a little.

Line 5

This has a different movement, although the vowels are quite long the first half of the line moves quite quickly to give space for those last three words – 'quite, quite, down!'

Line 6

Here the stress falls on the right words but we need that little moment, an early caesura perhaps, on the word 'I', plus in contrast to the open vowel sounds we have the grating sounds of 'deject' and 'wretched'.

Line 7

These grating sounds carry into the word 'sucked' – they imply inner disquiet – but soon turn into the smoothness of 'honey', 'music vows'.

Line 8

A regular line with quite even long vowels – 'see', 'noble', 'reason'.

Line 9

But here it begins to get more grating with 'jangled, out of tune and harsh'.

Line 10

And here it starts to go wild with 'blown youth'.

Line 11

This is where the whole speech is leading: the rhythm is broken immediately on that word 'blasted' which cannot be negotiated – it is a savage word – and it tells us all about her state of mind. It is as if she has been struck down the middle with lightning: here surely is where her madness starts. The line ends with those long vowels – 'woe is me'.

Line 12

This line with its long vowels, rounds it all up. She is mourning her loss: she is keening.

I will come back to this speech when we work through the strategies, but it would be good to finish off the exercise here by letting the group walk round in the space speaking it as they want, and exploring it in their own way. It is so important that they find their own connection with the images.

Anger and Resistance within the Language

For this I want to take a soliloquy of Leontes which comes in the second scene of *The Winter's Tale*. It is a speech in which he finds the words to express his jealousy of his friend Polixenes, unfounded of course, who he believes has won the affection of his wife Hermione. He sends them off to walk round the garden, and as he watches them go he starts to speak his thoughts. Although Mamilius, his son, is with him, it counts as a soliloquy for you feel the boy is neither listening nor understanding.

It is an amazing speech to work on because, as we speak it, we hear so clearly how one thought triggers the next, and how from small beginnings – 'Inch-thick, knee-deep...' we reach the hugeness of – 'It is a bawdy planet...': his jealousy is self-feeding – it is also global in size. Interestingly, if we read the first scene between Camillo and Archidemus we will hear how their over-rich and sensual language takes us into this world of Bohemia, and makes Leontes' jealousy completely plausible.

LEONTES: Gone already!
Inch-thick, knee-deep, o'er head and ears a forked one!
Go play, boy, play: thy mother plays, and I
Play too – but so disgraced a part, whose issue
Will hiss me to my grave. Contempt and clamour
Will be my knell. Go play, boy, play. There have been,
Or I am much deceived, cuckolds ere now;
And many a man there is, even at this present,

64

> Now, while I speak this, holds his wife by th'arm,
> That little thinks she has been sluiced in's absence,
> And his pond fished by his next neighbour, by
> Sir Smile, his neighbour. Nay, there's comfort in't
> Whiles other men have gates, and those gates opened,
> As mine, against their will. Should all despair
> That have revolted wives, the tenth of mankind
> Would hang themselves. Physic for't there's none:
> It is a bawdy planet, that will strike
> Where 'tis predominant; and 'tis powerful, think it,
> From east, west, north, and south. Be it concluded,
> No barricado for a belly. Know't:
> It will let in and out the enemy
> With bag and baggage. Many thousand on's
> Have the disease and feel't not. How now,boy?[1]

The text is not difficult to understand, but the structure and the images are complex, and the group will need time for it to lie with them.

- So let them walk round speaking it through a couple of times for themselves: then gather them and let them speak it through together.

- They will find a lot to say about the words used, very potent and sexual – eg,
  'inch-thick, knee-deep – a fork'd one'
  'play' – with its triple meaning – 'Go play, boy, play…' – ie, the boy's 'play' which is innocent,
  'thy mother plays' – with its sexual connotation;
  'And I play too' – referring to his own game-playing to catch them out by sending them into the garden.

- The words are ugly –
  'hiss me to my grave' – 'contempt and clamour' – 'cuckolds' – and those words –
  'sluic'd', 'and his pond fish'd'

---

1   *The Winter's Tale*, I ii.

– with their implications of the sexual act in a deeply derogatory and degrading way. The thoughts are self-feeding, they grow from that first image –
'inch-thick' into – 'a bawdy planet'
until we get to –
'From east, west, north and south. Be it concluded
No barricado for a belly.'

It is truly an amazing speech: in a short time we can of course only scratch the surface, but it can make us aware of so much.

When they are ready, we want first to hear how the thoughts move – and here I mean whole thoughts, not just punctuation marks.

- To do this get them to go to different parts of the space and speak one thought, then move somewhere else and speak the next thought. It is important to keep still when speaking and only move between thoughts. What we will hear is the relentless restlessness of his thinking, how his mind is constantly on the move and feeding his central theme.

- Next, they should take time to beat the metre through once. They will find how so many of the lines are over full and need negotiating, and so many have a feminine ending, ie, an extra unstressed syllable at the end of a line, as thus –

>   'whose issue
> Will hiss me to my grave. Contempt and clamour
> Will be my knell.'

- And then hear the fullness of the following –

>   'the tenth of mankind
> Would hang themselves. Physic for't there's none...'

- The word 'physic' just jumps out at you: or –

>   'that will strike
> Where 'tis predominant; and 'tis powerful, think it...'

- Those words 'predominant' and 'powerful' are strong and take time to speak.

- It is such marvellously physical language to play around with, which comes to its head with –

  'No barricado for a belly...'

- Which carries with it a certain absurdity: and from there it deteriorates into –

  'With bag and baggage...'

- It is as if he cannot find enough words to satisfy the depth of his feelings.

Lastly we need to hear how the very jaggedness of the thoughts comes from his resistance to express them: the thoughts hurt in a savage way. so we need to find that resistance.

- You will need a volunteer to read the speech through once, someone who is fairly comfortable with reading it.
- Then get the reader, Leontes, to stand in the middle of the space with the rest of the group surrounding him or her.
- As 'Leontes' speaks it through he or she must try to get out of the circle and cross to the other side of the room, or even out of the door. The resistance the actor will find is akin to the difficulty Leontes has in uttering his thoughts – they hurt.

The group will have to be sensible and not get too rough so that the actor reading has a chance of getting through – but they will all hear how that resistance affects the physicality of the language and the extraordinary wildness and anarchy of his thoughts – they are just not reasonable or reasoned: he is consumed with jealousy – it is a kind of madness. The actor reading Leontes will feel this anarchy and stress in the body, and this will give it a different charge of energy.

If preferred, the same work can be done on the speech of Paulina in the same play:

PAULINA: What studied torments, tyrant, hast for me?
            What wheels? Racks? Fires? What flaying? Boiling

In leads or oils? What old or newer torture
Must I receive, whose every word deserves
To taste of thy most worst? Thy tyranny,
Together working with thy jealousies –
Fancies too weak for boys, too green and idle
For girls of nine – O think what they have done,
And then run mad indeed, stark mad! For all
Thy bygone fooleries were but spices of it.
That thou betrayedst Polixines 'twas nothing:
That did but show thee of a fool inconstant,
And damnable ingrateful. Nor was't much
Thou wouldst have poisoned good Camillo's honour
To have him kill a king – poor trespasses,
More monstrous standing by: whereof I reckon
The casting forth to crows thy baby daughter
To be or none or little, though a devil
Would have shed water out of fire ere done't;
Nor is't directly laid to thee, the death
Of the young Prince, whose honourable thoughts –
Thoughts high for one so tender – cleft the heart,
That could conceive a gross and foolish sire
Blemished his gracious dam. This is not, no,
Laid to thy answer. But the last – O lords,
When I have said, cry woe! The Queen, the Queen,
The sweet'st, dear'st, creature's dead! And vengeance
  for't
Not dropped down yet.[1]

Her anger at Leontes is unleashed through this speech, and her underlying need to make him see reason and relent: her deep disgust at his treatment of Hermione is manifest in the rhythm of her utterance, and you hear the challenge which underpins it.

I always like to end up with a piece of modern text so that we see how the work connects with the language of today. I very often use the following speech from Edward Bond's *Lear*. Also, because

---

1 *The Winter's Tale*, III ii.

it is in prose, we see how the exercises work equally well for prose as for verse. It is by no means easy to understand, but by using some of the work that we have been exploring on the movement of thoughts and the physicality of the language, we immediately begin to grasp some of the passion and the pity in Lear.

> LEAR: The king is always on oath! (*He stares down at the mirror.*) No, that's not the king… This is a little cage of bars with an animal in it. (*Peers closer.*) No, no that's not the king! (*Suddenly gestures violently. The USHER takes the mirror.*) Who shut that animal in that cage? Let it out. Have you seen its face behind the bars? There's a poor animal with blood on its head and tears running down its face. Who did that to it? Is it a bird or a horse? It's lying in the dust and its wings are broken. Who broke its wings? Who cut off its hands so that it can't shake the bars? It's pressing its snout on the glass. Who shut that animal in a glass cage? O God, there's no pity in this world. You let it lick the blood from its hair in the corner of a cage with nowhere to hide from its tormentors. No shadow, no hole! Let that animal out of its cage! (*He takes the mirror and shows it round.*) Look! Look! Have pity. Look at its claws trying to open the cage. It's dragging its broken body over the floor. You are cruel! Cruel! Look at it lying in its corner! It's shocked and cut and shaking and licking the blood on its sides. (*USHER again takes the mirror from LEAR.*) No, no! Where are they taking it now! Not out of my sight! What will they do to it? O God, give it to me! Let me hold it and stroke it and wipe its blood! (*BODICE takes the mirror from the USHER.*) No![1]

- For this amazing speech, get the group to read it through on their own several times – not listening to each other.

- Then let them start to walk around the space while reading it in their own time.

- Carry on with this, but now get them to turn sharply on each punctuation mark.

---

1 *Lear*, Act 2 Scene 1. Edward Bond, *Plays Two* (Eyre Methuen: London, 1978), 49.

- By doing this we will begin to hear and feel that incredible rhythm which transmits the sense of an animal being caged, and the cruelty involved.

About the Workshop

In this workshop we have covered a great deal of ground and have dealt with many of the issues regarding the structure that we will be looking at in detail in the next chapter: how the language takes us into the world of the play, and how the texture of the language informs the subtextual meaning.

Now in rehearsal, when an exercise has been successful for the actor by opening out, perhaps, a deeper understanding of the character, and a way of expressing that through the language, the question from the actor will always be – 'How can I retain that feeling, that charge, while playing the scene on stage when probably standing quite still?'. The answer I think has to be that once you have found that other understanding, something which one has felt through the whole of one's body, that awareness will always be there at the centre to give you that extra hold on the character, and you just have to be patient while you allow that to be absorbed into the character.

As I have said, this workshop covers quite a large spread of work, and you may not get through it all completely, but what is important is that everyone has an experience of speaking this language through in a group, and of enjoying its diversity. We now have to look at how this work can be used to serve the rehearsal process itself.

Chapter Four

GROUP WORK ON FORM AND STRUCTURE

MY MAIN FOCUS in this chapter is on the practical issues of form, structure and rhythm, and also the texture of the language, in order to discover how they all directly inform our exploration of character. Much of this we looked at in the workshop so I will be referring back to that a good deal. It is work that can be done either on the text in rehearsal, or on other texts which are similar in style – whichever is most useful. At the end of this chapter (page 99), I will look at what I call 'the word itself', and suggest three ways to help us to keep exploring the words afresh.

I want to say here that, because I have come to these ways of exploring text via Shakespeare, as that has been my main source of work for the last thirty years or more, my focus in the book is on his text. But I do again stress that all the work can be used equally well for all periods of dramatic writing, be it Jacobean, Restoration, 21st century, etc. Somehow, because he was able to capture the speech rhythms of people even within his most heightened language, and though the actual words we use today may be different, the sense we get out of the rhythm stays with us still, and so his writing illustrates clearly and simply the points one wants to make. It most definitely sharpens our awareness to the possibilities of rhythm and cadence more than any other dramatic writing I know. Although we are focusing here on the basic form of the text, this will not limit the possibilities; rather it will make us free to hear the infinite variety within its form. There is always anarchy and surprise hidden there in its sound.

The Practical Issues

As I see it there are six basic issues at the centre of the work on every play, be it Shakespeare or 21st century or anything in between, which we need to address so that they become totally integrated with motive and character – in other words, a living part of the spoken text.

   i Hearing where the language takes us:
      how we enter that other world, and that other character, through the choice of the word itself.

  ii The rhythm and movement of thought:
      if in prose, how the rhythm and phrasing tells us so much about the emotional state of the character. If in verse, the variety of movement within a verse line whilst negotiating sense stress and metre stress, and how the association of different vowels and consonants affect this. This also includes the possibility of a caesura – a break in the verse line.

 iii Language textures:
      vowel and consonant lengths within a line.

 iv Speech structures:
      how the particular format of a speech can evoke a reaction from the listener – we can be moved to tears or laughter by its very form. Plus how we lay the thoughts – ie, the spaces needed for those thoughts to land: this is crucial in order for the audience to take in all the ideas and nuances within the writing, without overstressing or pressurising. And also hear how the cadences of sound which are possible: this can be quite minimal, because of course we do not want any extravagance, however we do want subtly to signal the changes of direction in the thought. Plus it is these often minimal changes in pitch which draw in the listener and awaken their curiosity – in the end, we are bored by flat speech.

  v Where the image lies:
      the images in a play are not just pictures, they tell us where the character is living within themselves.

vi The word itself.

The World of the Play

As put forward in the workshop, it is so important right at the beginning to get in touch with the language of the play, and hear where it takes us. This goes for any play, be the writing classical or modern.

- So, as soon as possible when rehearsals begin, we need to get the cast to sit round in a circle and read the first scene, or part of the scene, together – not taking particular roles, but reading a speech or part of a speech in turn.

- Let the group read it, without trying to interpret it or make decisions about it – simply listening to the text as it is being read. They can do this a couple of times if necessary so that any difficulty re the meaning can be clarified.

- Then allot the parts, not necessarily as they are cast, and as it is read through again, ask the rest of the group to mutter words that grab them in some way – each person will respond differently.

- Only those who are reading can look at the script, the others should simply listen, so that the text is heard away from the words on the page. Our consciousness is then tuned into the language, and we become aware of the specificity of the words to that place, that situation and that character.

What is important about this is that it not only feeds our imagination, but it also takes us subconsciously into that 'other' place, that 'other' awareness, and this will lay on the hearer without anything being consciously stressed. In other words, it gets us ready for the world and the situation that is to come. That world is then transmitted through the actor to the audience, not by emphasising anything or being knowing about it, but simply by being with the words.

The two plays we looked at in the workshop session were perhaps rather clear examples in that the subtext in both is so palpable, and the texts are straightforward in structure – although I do think it is always surprising how dark that world of the *Dream* is. Plays such as *The Winter's Tale* with its opulence and sexual word play, or *Measure for Measure* with its convoluted argument and almost legal language, are more difficult to pin down, but it is so important that we take time to hear that language and that world, and feel part of it.

It is particularly useful to do this work on Jacobean plays, where the structure of the language is complex and very formal. The actor needs to get used to that formality so that it becomes part of their natural world and, as in the first scene of Webster's *The White Devil* for instance, we hear the world of corruption and of murder, a world that lacks all pity. We have that wonderful line of Lodovico, when Gasparo tries to comfort him on his banishment, he replies –

> Leave your painted comforts.
> I'll make Italian cut-works in their guts
> If ever I return.[1]

What an image: making fancy embroidery or lace out of some-one's guts – opulence and cruelty in one sentence. Now the more at ease the actor is with that extravagance the more truly it will be expressed, and therefore the more the audience will believe in that world. They will then become involved in the reality of the story as of now, and not as something which can be observed at one remove. We do not want the audience to 'appreciate it' as they listen – we want them to believe it. This first scene of *The White Devil* is a great piece to work on, to find the convoluted structure of the language, which in turn takes us into the rich world of the Italian nobility, albeit cruel and lascivious.

There is also the first scene of *King Lear*, where he asks each of his daughters how much they love him so that he can decide how much land to give them. Both Goneril and Regan go overboard in expressing how much they love him, and he rewards them accordingly. But when it comes to Cordelia and he asks –

---

1 John Webster, *The White Devil*, I i.

LEAR:	What can you say to draw
	A third more opulent than your sisters'? Speak!
CORDELIA:	Nothing, my lord.
LEAR:	Nothing?
CORDELIA:	Nothing.
LEAR:	Nothing can come of nothing...[1]

We have been taken immediately into Lear's mixed-up world of somehow quantifying love and equating it with property: it is all about 'how much', be it property or love. Does his madness spring from this?

It is of course totally different in modern writing, where the exchanges between characters can often be quite minimal, but in its way it is just as palpable, for though the words may be few, they place us in that world. Pinter's *The Homecoming* is a wonderful example –

What have you done with the scissors?[2]

It is perfectly simple to understand, but just by repeating the word 'scissors' they become part of that establishment in a different way. It is an amazing beginning to the play, seemingly very ordinary, but as the scene continues, and as the father reminisces about his old friend Mac, about his wife, about horse-racing, and by the very sparseness of the dialogue between father and son, we become aware of their aloneness and their lack of communication, and our curiosity is immediately aroused about the world they have created for themselves. It is the detail in the dialogue which creates the world.

And that is the delight: if at the beginning of the rehearsal period you spend a little time simply listening to the text, without trying to interpret it but hearing where it takes you, the communication between the actors becomes that much richer. So much of modern writing is in the rhythm, and often short-cut phrasing. You only

---

1 *King Lear*, I i.
2 Harold Pinter, *The Homecoming*, Act One.

have to look at the beginning of *Blasted* by Sarah Kane to get a taste of her very bleak world. The first three utterances are:

IAN: I've shat in better places than this.

        (He gulps down the gin.)

        I stink.
        You want a bath?

CATE: *(Shakes her head.)*

        (IAN goes into the bathroom and we hear him run the water. He comes back in with only a towel around his waist and a revolver In his hand. He checks it is loaded and puts it under his pillow.)

IAN: Tip that wog when he brings up the sandwiches.

        (He leaves fifty pence and goes into the bathroom.
        CATE comes further into the room.
        She puts her bag down and bounces on the bed.
        She goes around the room, looking in every drawer, touching everything.
        She smells the flowers and smiles.)

CATE: Lovely.[1]

It does not have to be stressed, but it has to feed our awareness.
  In her author's note at the beginning Kane says:

> Punctuation is used to indicate delivery, not to conform to the rules of grammar.

Surely that is just the point: the writer writes the rhythm of the character's thoughts, and how better to get to know that character than in the spaces between the thoughts.

---

1 *Blasted*, Scene One. Sarah Kane, *Complete Plays* (Methuen Drama: London, 2001), 3–4.

The delight is that every play has a different world, be it Beckett, Tennessee Williams, Arnold Wesker, and although when the curtain goes up we see a picture of that world on the stage, it is through the dialogue that we enter its heart. This first scene from Timberlake Wertenbaker's *Our Country's Good* does just that.

Scene One. The Voyage out

The hold of a convict ship bound for Australia, 1787.
The convicts huddle together in the semi-darkness. On
deck, the convict ROBIN SIDEWAY is being flogged. Second
Lieutenant RALPH CLARK counts the lashes in a barely
audible, slow and monotonous voice.

RALPH CLARK: Forty-four, forty-five, forty-six, forty-seven, forty-eight, forty-nine, fifty.

SIDEWAY is untied and dumped with the rest of the
convicts. He collapses. No one moves. A short silence.

JOHN WISEHAMMER: At night? The sea cracks against the ship. Fear whispers, screams, falls silent, hushed. Spewed from our country, forgotten, bound to the dark edge of the earth, at night what is there to do but seek English cunt, warm, moist, soft, oh the comfort, the comfort of the lick, the thrust into the nooks, the crannies of the crooks of England. Alone, frightened, nameless in this stinking hole of hell, take me, take me inside you, whoever you are. Take me, my comfort and we'll remember England together.

JOHN ARSCOTT: Hunger. Funny. Doesn't start in the stomach, but in the mind. A picture flits in and out of a corner. Something you have eaten long ago. Roast beef with salt and grated horseradish.

MARY BRENHAM: I don't know why I did it. Love, I suppose.[1]

As you will see this work is useful for modern writing, where the first scenes are so often monosyllabic and enigmatic, arousing our

---

1 *Our Country's Good*, Scene One. Timberlake Wertenbaker, *Plays One* (Faber & Faber: London, 1996), 185.

curiosity about the world we are entering: again in Mark Ravenhill's *Shopping and Fucking*, we are taken into a world which is questioning whether there is anything left in our lives that cannot be bought and sold.

MARK: Yes. OK.
It's summer. I'm in a supermarket. It's hot and I'm sweaty. Damp. And I'm watching this couple shopping. I'm watching you. And you're both smiling. You see me and you know sort of straight away that I'm going to have you. You know you don't have a choice. No control. Now this guy comes up to me. He's a fat man. Fat and hair and lycra and he says:
See the pair by the yoghurt?
Well, says fat guy, they're both mine. I own them. I own them but I don't want them – because you know something? – they're trash. Trash and I hate them. Wanna buy them? How much?
Piece of trash like them. Let's say…twenty. Yeah, yours for twenty.
So, I do the deal. I hand it over. And I fetch you. I don't have to say anything because you know. You've seen the transaction.
And I take you both away and I take you to my house. And you see the house and when you see the house you know it. You understand? You know this place. And I've been keeping a room for you and I take you into this room. And there's food. And it's warm. And we live out our days fat and content and happy.[1]

The Rhythm and Movement of Thought in both Verse and Prose

As we found in the workshop, moving on punctuation is a very positive way to discover how the thoughts of a character are not just a

---

1 *Shopping and Fucking*, Scene 1. Mark Ravenhill, *Plays One* (Methuen Drama: London, 2001), 5.

series of connecting phrases which make literal sense, but in their very rhythm are an expression of the whole self, the body as well as the mind. This was made clear when reading the speeches of Egeus (page 52), Leontes (page 64) and Paulina (page 68): the way the thoughts moved reflected the extreme agitation within themselves. Plus the speech from Bond's *Lear* (page 69) made us feel something of the state of cruelty and destruction within that world.

So, with the text in rehearsal, you can get each of the actors to read a section of their own part of the text, walking around and changing direction on the punctuation marks.

- By doing this they will tune into the movement of the thoughts, and how that movement is integral to the mental and emotional state of the character. This can be done singly, or they can just do it altogether around in the space; they will still hear what is happening in their own text and feel the rhythm within themselves.

The speeches I have listed so far have all been rather explosive and angry, but this exercise can be equally helpful for texts which are quite thoughtful, exploring ideas or feelings, such as Theseus in the *Dream* (IV ii), which begins –

> More strange than true. I never may believe
> These antique fables, nor these fairy toys.
> Lovers and madmen have such seething brains,
> Such shaping fantasies, that apprehend
> More than cool reason ever comprehends.
> The lunatic, the lover, and the poet
> Are of imagination all compact...

As he goes on to consider how we are affected by our imagination, so his thoughts move to different parts of himself until he reaches a conclusion.

What is important is that it makes us realise how our thoughts are part of our whole self and not just the mind, and that speaking them is always an action. We speak them in order to provoke a further thought or a further response, either from ourselves or from the other person. In any one play, I believe there is never a full-stop until the last word is spoken, and this can be equally applied to Jimmy Porter in *Look Back in Anger*, or Blanche in *A Streetcar Named Desire*. Thoughts are always active in that they make us discover more about ourselves.

Verse Rhythms

If working on Shakespeare, or any of the Elizabethan and Jacobean plays, it is important to take a little time to listen to the iambic rhythm and how it fits into a line. So much has been written about the iambic pentameter and I think there are many actors, particularly the younger ones, who feel that there are rules to be followed and a 'right' way of speaking it. So it is always good to clear the way right at the beginning, for the choice in the end lies with the actor.

In the workshop session we looked in detail at how metre and sense interacted on several texts – Sonnet 129 (page 38), Junius Brutus from *Coriolanus* (page 56) and Ophelia (page 61) – and how, because of varying vowel and consonant lengths, we realised that each line has its own movement within it.

- So take a piece of text and beat it through together in strict rhythm as you speak it.

- It will fall into five beats – ten syllables, consisting of five unstressed and five stressed syllables: te-tum te-tum te-tum te-tum te-tum. There may also be an extra syllable at the end of a line which is unstressed (this is called a feminine ending).

- As you do this you will notice how the metre stress falls with the sense stress – sometimes in agreement and sometimes not.

- Having experienced that basic metre and where it falls the actor will realise that there is always negotiation to be done, in order –
  i to make the sense clear, and
  ii to give full value to the words – ie, their length and texture.

You have only to look at this speech of Capulet in *Romeo and Juliet*, to hear the possible vagaries of the iambic beat:

CAPULET: How, how, how, how, chopped logic? What is this?
          'Proud' – and 'I thank you' – and 'I thank you not' –
          And yet 'not proud'? Mistress minion you,
          Thank me no thankings, nor proud me no prouds,
          But fettle your fine joints 'gainst Thursday next
          To go with Paris to Saint Peter's Church,
          Or I will drag thee on a hurdle thither.
          Out, you green-sickness carrion! Out, you baggage!
          You tallow-face![1]

And this is what is exciting, for each actor will hear the text slightly differently, and have their own preference for the balancing of the sense itself: this is what the actor needs to play with and enjoy. Yet the underlying beat holds firm, just as in jazz. I also think it important at a later stage in rehearsal to urge actors to go through one or two of their own speeches beating out the metre for themselves. When you check on the metre in this way after you have worked on the play a little, you will often hear things that both surprise and add to your perception of the character.

Then of course there is the caesura. As we have seen, this is simply a momentary break, or space in the middle of a verse line – or, to repeat Edith Evans' term, 'poise'. That word 'poise' is so apposite, for the caesura is not a pause, nor does it break up the line: rather it is a moment of suspense, a word that you hold for that split moment, in order for the listener to be ready, or hungry, for what is to come. It always lifts you and makes you ready for the rest of the line and thought.

Certain research done on the art of rhetoric tells us that there are only so many words that the listener can take in at one time without a moment to allow the sense to drop in. In verse we so often need that moment of space mid-line to lay the salient word – the word that has to be laid in our thoughts. Not every line has a caesura, that would not be interesting, but we must always be open to its possibility and use it when it is there. The sense so often lies in the spaces.

---

1 *Romeo and Juliet*, III v.

In Shakespeare's early plays, although on the whole they are rhythmically quite regular and it is usual for the thoughts to be rounded off at the end of a line, there is so often that momentary lift on a word mid-line, as in the first two lines of *The Two Gentlemen of Verona* (I i):

> Cease to persuade, my loving Proteus;
> Home-keeping youth have ever homely wits...

- We need that lift on 'persuade' so that 'my loving Proteus' can drop in and we become aware of something of the friendship between the two characters.

- And again on the second line we need to let those first words drop in so we get the reasoning of the whole line, for this sets up the theme of the play.

Or take these famous lines of John of Gaunt from *Richard II* –

> This royal throne of kings, this sceptred isle,
> This earth of majesty, this seat of Mars,
> This other Eden – demi-paradise –
> This fortress built by nature for herself
> Against infection and the hand of war...[1]

As you will hear, the first three lines have a caesura in the middle – ie, at 'kings', 'majesty', and 'Eden' – while the last two lines do not have a break, so the rhythm is quite different, and it is that variation which keeps our ears alert.

However in the later plays so often the full-stop lies mid-line, as with Junius Brutus' speech from *Coriolanus* that we have already looked at (page 56) –

> All tongues speak of him and the bleared sights
> Are spectacled to see him. Your prattling nurse
> Into a rapture lets her baby cry
> While she chats him. The kitchen malkin pins

---

1 *Richard II*, II i.

> Her richest lockram 'bout her reechy neck
> Clamb'ring the walls to eye him. Stalls, bulks,
> windows...[1]

This is a particularly good example of the caesura, for so many of the breaks are on the word 'him', which of course highlights Brutus' contempt for Coriolanus. The third and fifth lines are smooth and expansive in thought as he feeds his anger with his images. But that break never holds the line up; rather, that momentary poise allows us to move on the last half of the line more quickly and lift it, always giving the feeling that there is more to come.

Another good piece to look at is Camillo's speech in the second scene of *The Winter's Tale*: Leontes has just confided in him his suspicion that Hermione is unfaithful; he also accuses Camillo of being untrustworthy. Camillo is so taken aback that he can hardly get his thoughts together, and we hear his initial confusion in the broken rhythms of the first part of the speech:

CAMILLO: My gracious lord,
> I may be negligent, foolish and fearful:
> In every one of these no man is free,
> But that his negligence, his folly, fear,
> Among the infinite doings of the world,
> Sometimes puts forth. In your affairs, my lord,
> If ever I were wilful-negligent,
> It was my folly; if industriously
> I played the fool, it was my negligence
> Not weighing well the end; if ever fearful
> To do a thing where I the issue doubted,
> Whereof the execution did cry out
> Against the non-performance, 'twas a fear
> Which oft infects the wisest. These, my lord,
> Are such allowed infirmities that honesty
> Is never free of. But, beseech your grace,
> Be plainer with me, let me know my trespass

---

1 *Coriolanus*, II i.

By its own visage; if I then deny it,
'Tis none of mine.[1]

This is a good example of how the thoughts are invented; we hear through the rhythm the way Camillo has to twist and turn as he finds his way through a very difficult situation, and how he clarifies his argument as he goes. Only in the last four lines does he find some form of resolution.

The more texts we look at the more we will discover that there is just an infinite variety of play between that basic rhythm and the sense you want to convey. This variety is enriched by the very texture of the language – ie, the length of vowels, and the length and number of consonants. This is what is so stimulating, for it is like jazz, or blues, or reggae, where the singer has endless freedom to play with the basic beat: in Shakespeare the choice is with the actor. But, like the beat of the music, there is the basic time of that iambic pentameter which has to be honoured: that is what gives the language its bottom-line energy and suspense. And of course there is Ophelia's speech that we have already looked at (page 61), which is a wonderful example of how a jaggedness, a break in the rhythm, can convey so strongly the inner state of the character.

Prose Rhythms

That inner state which is made apparent by the rhythm and the movement of a verse line, is just as palpable in prose, but perhaps more difficult to define. To find how the rhythm informs the under-lying meaning it is good to do the following.

- First, in a circle, take a piece of text and let the group read it through together.

- Then they need to read the text in the circle with each person reading one phrase – ie, each person reads to the next punc-tuation mark: this way we hear the rhythm of the thoughts themselves. It is important that as they read they do not try to

---

1   *The Winter's Tale*, I ii.

interpret it or convey the underlying motive which they perceive is there – simply speak the text quite straight so that the length and rhythm of the phrases become absolutely apparent: the important thing for them is to hear the spaces in between the punctuation marks – the spaces in the text.

- You can then hear how the rhythm itself carries the essence of both the meaning and the underlying emotion.

This is very helpful nowadays, when we tend to emphasise the emotional undertones, and perhaps over-explain them. We need to hear afresh how the rhythm of the text is absolutely specific and integral to the state of the character – and is moving of itself. The speech of the Hostess in *Henry V* is a powerful example of this:

BARDOLPH: Would I were with him, wheresome'er he is, either in heaven or in hell!

HOSTESS: Nay, sure, he's not in hell: he's in Arthur's bosom, if ever man went to Arthur's bosom. 'A made a finer end, and went away an it had been any christom child; 'a parted e'en just between twelve and one, e'en at the turning o'th'tide; for after I saw him fumble with the sheets, and play with flowers, and smile upon his fingers' ends, I knew there was but one way; for his nose was as sharp as a pen, and 'a babbled of green fields. 'How now, Sir John?' quoth I, 'What, man, be o' good cheer!' So 'a cried out, 'God, God, God!' three or four times. Now I, to comfort him, bid him 'a should not think of God – I hoped there was no need to trouble himself with any such thoughts yet. So 'a bade me lay more clothes on his feet; I put my hand into the bed, and felt them, and they were as cold as any stone; then I felt to his knees, and so up'ard and up'ard, and all was as cold as any stone.[1]

These are Falstaff's last moments as she remembers them and she seems quite objective about it, as we often are when talking about something which touches us deeply, but it is in the rhythm and in the spaces, that we hear the poignancy of the moment. At the

---

1   *Henry V,* II i.

beginning she gives us the facts, she then goes on to describe very specifically each moment – precise in every detail –

> after I saw him fumble with the sheets,
> and play with flowers,
> and smile upon his fingers' ends,
> I knew there was but one way;

And then at the end – when she puts her hands into the bed and feels how cold he is, each moment is given its space –

> So 'a bade me lay more clothes on his feet;
> I put my hand into the bed,
> and felt them,
> and they were as cold as any stone;
> then I felt to his knees,
> and so up'ard and up'ard,
> and all was as cold as any stone.

There is something in the precision of the words and in the rhythm which is deeply moving: it does not have to be coloured with feeling, that belittles it – that feeling is embodied in the rhythm itself.

There is that same precision as Jimmy Porter remembers his father's death in *Look Back in Anger*, pouring out all that was left of his life to no-one,

JIMMY: Anyone who's never watched somebody die is suffering from a pretty bad case of virginity. *(His good humour of a moment ago deserts him, as he begins to remember.)* For twelve months, I watched my father dying – when I was ten years old. He'd come back from the war In Spain, you see. And certain God-fearing gentlemen there had made such a mess of him, he didn't have long left to live. Everyone knew it – even I knew it. *(He moves R.)* But, you see, I was the only one who cared. *(Turns to window.)* His family were embarrassed by the whole business. Embarrassed and irritated. *(Looking out.)* As for my mother, all she could think about was the fact that she had allied herself to a man who semed to be on the wrong side in all things. My mother

86

was all for being associated with minorities, provided they were the smart, fashionable ones. *(He moves up C. again.)* We all of us waited for him to die. The family sent him a cheque every month, and hoped he'd get on with it quietly, without too much vulgar fuss. My mother looked after him without complaining, and that was about all. Perhaps she pitied him. I suppose she was capable of that. *(With a kind of appeal in his voice.)* But *I* was the only one who cared! *(He moves L., behind the armchair.)* Every time I sat on the edge of his bed, to listen to him talking or reading to me, I had to fight back my tears. At the end of twelve months, I was a veteran. *(He leans forward on the back of the armchair.)* All that that feverish failure of a man had to listen to him was a small, frightened boy. I spent hour upon hour in that tiny bedroom. He would talk to me for hours, pouring out what was left of his life to one, lonely, bewildered little boy, who could barely understand half of what he said. All he could feel was the despair and the bitterness, the sweet, sickly smell of a dying man. *(He moves round the chair.)* You see, I learnt at an early age what it was to be angry – angry and helpless. And I can never forget it. *(Sits.)* I knew more about – love…betrayal…and death, when I was ten years old than you will probably ever know all your life.[1]

It is certainly very moving, and revealing.

As I said at the beginning when I quoted Johnny Beattie, the same applies to comedy. How often, when we listen to one of Shakespeare's comedic characters – Touchstone or Feste for example – do we laugh at a speech without perhaps fully understanding its content? For it is in the different lengths of the phrases and the spaces in between that the humour is released.

We can take an example from Shaw, the Devil's speech in *Man and Superman*: the dark ironic humour in this speech is compounded by the rhythm, and the varied lengths of the phrases. If you try to explain the speech by breaking it up into smaller phrases, we

---

1 *Look Back in Anger*, Act Two Scene One. John Osborne, *Plays One* (Faber & Faber: London, 1996), 55–6.

87

will not get the whole picture, the whole message. He begins by asking –

And is Man any the less destroying himself for all this boasted brain of his?[1]

He then argues his point through for nearly three pages – here are the last few lines:

The plague, the famine, the earthquake, the tempest were too spasmodic in their action; the tiger and the crocodile were too easily satiated and not cruel enough: something more constantly, more ruthlessly, more ingeniously destructive was needed; and that something was Man, the inventor of the rack, the stake, the gallows, the electric chair; of sword and gun and poison gas; above all, of justice, duty, patriotism, and all the other isms by which even those who are clever enough to be humanely disposed are persuaded to become the most destructive of all the destroyers.[2]

There is something very stimulating to the ear about the whole speech, the questions he asks, the debate which is always provoking a response: we are excited by its very rhythm. This is of course particularly relevant to modern text which is predominantly in prose, and where the world is conveyed in the rhythm of the character speaking – Beckett, Williams, Ravenhill, Carr.

So, whatever text you are working, classical or modern, always take time to experiment with the rhythm and so discover the underlying heartbeat – humorous or sad. Here are two examples of humour, both from *Troilus and Cressida*. First, Thersites (II iii):

THERSITES: How now, Thersites! What, lost in the labyrinth of thy fury? Shall the elephant Ajax carry it thus? He beats me, and I rail at him: O, worthy satisfaction! Would it were otherwise – that I could beat him whilst he railed at me. 'Sfoot, I'll learn to

---

1 George Bernard Shaw, *Man and Superman* (Penguin Books: Harmondsworth, 2000), 142.
2 *Man and Superman*, 144.

conjure and raise devils, but I'll see some issue of my spiteful
execrations. Then there's Achilles – a rare engineer. If Troy be not
taken till these two undermine it, the walls will stand till they fall
of themselves. O thou great thunder-darter of Olympus, forget
that thou art Jove, the king of gods; and Mercury, lose all the
serpentine craft of thy caduceus, if thou take not that little little,
less than little wit from them that they have! – which short-
armed ignorance itself knows is so abundant scarce it will not in
circumvention deliver a fly from a spider without drawing their
massy irons and cutting the web. After this, the vengeance on
the whole camp – or rather, the Neapolitan bone-ache – for that,
methinks, is the curse dependent on those that war for a placket.
I have said my prayers, and devil Envy say 'Amen'.

We hear the underlying fury in this speech through the vola-
tile rhythm and the viciousness of the imagery as he rails against
Ajax, Achilles and the gods. From it we get the whole sense of the
corruption within this world – the Neapolitan bone-ache, or syphi-
lis, which pervades: it is the world in which Cressida exists.

Then this from Pandarus (III ii), as he seals the bargain made
between Troilus and Cressida:

PANDARUS: Go to, a bargain made; seal it, seal it, I'll be the witness.
Here I hold your hand, here my cousin's. If ever you prove false
one to another, since I have taken such pains to bring you
together, let all pitiful goers-between be called to the world's
end after my name; call them all Pandars. Let all constant men be
called Troiluses, all false women Cressids, and all brokers-between
Pandars! Say 'Amen'.

This is smoother in rhythm than Thersites' speech, but there is
something in its movement which tells of the worldly irony which
underlies his thinking. We do not have to stress that irony, for if we
do it becomes predictable and knowing: just find the rhythm and
the humour will come through, dark though it may be.

Language Textures

This variety of movement within any verse line is not only dependent on the sense and how it works with the metre, it is also dependent on the length of the vowel sounds, the number of consonants, and whether those consonants are predominantly voiced or unvoiced. This is obvious I know, but it is important that we tune into the possibilities – for instance the difference between –

ANGELO: What's this? What's this? Is this her fault or mine?
The tempter or the tempted, who sins most?[1]

and –

CORDELIA: Alack, 'tis he! Why, he was met even now
As mad as the vexed sea, singing aloud,
Crowned with rank fumiter and furrow-weeds,
With hardokes, hemlock, nettles, cuckoo-flowers,
Darnel, and all the idle weeds that grow
In our sustaining corn. (*To SOLDIERS.*) A century send
  forth;
Search every acre of the high-grown field
And bring him to our eye. (*Exeunt SOLDIERS.*)
(*To DOCTOR.*)   What can man's wisdom
In the restoring his bereavèd sense?[2]

It is so important to hear the difference between the movement and sharpness of Angelo's lines – with its devoiced consonants and short vowels, which tell us of his frustration – and the length of Cordelia's vowels as she pictures her father in his madness.

But of course what is often difficult for the actor today is to give space to those long vowels and hear their pain without perhaps feeling a little false. A good way to free this is to take this speech of Titus Andronicus, and to experience a physical resistance as you speak the words.

TITUS: If there were reason for these miseries,

---

1 *Measure for Measure,* II i.
2 *King Lear,* IV iv.

Then into limits could I bind my woes.
When heaven doth weep, doth not the earth o'erflow?
If the winds rage, doth not the sea wax mad,
Threat'ning the welkin with his big-swoll'n face?
And wilt thou have a reason for this coil?
I am the sea. Hark how her sighs doth blow.
She is the weeping welkin, I the earth.
Then must my sea be movèd with her sighs,
Then must my earth with her continual tears
Become a deluge overflowed and drowned.
For why my bowels cannot hide her woes,
But like a drunkard must I vomit them.
Then give me leave, for losers will have leave
To ease their stomachs with their bitter tongues.[1]

It is such an amazing piece of writing, and there are two exercises
you can do on it.

ONE

- First let the group get into a circle read it through together
  a couple of times to get familiar with the language and the
  meaning.

- Now ask them to get into a circle and link arms very firmly, and
  as they read it through again, to pull against each other quite
  forcibly.

- They will then hear how this extreme physical action affects the
  speaking and lengthens out those vowels – yet it will not sound
  false.

TWO

- Ask them to find an object to kick, such as a shoe – something
  firm but not too big – and then get them to walk round speaking
  the text while kicking the object quite hard; they will bump into
  each other as they go.

---

1 *Titus Andronicus,* III i.

- In this way they will find the roughness and muscularity of the language without thinking about it, and be surprised by it.

These are slightly extreme exercises, but because they are extreme they heighten our awareness of the different textures in language, and how those textures reinforce the meaning. This sense of texture in language is equally true of modern writing, though of course in a less heightened style: and even in our everyday conversation when we are using words which are aligned to our situation in some way, this is reflected in the sound of the words we use. But of course that awareness has to impinge on the hearer subliminally, it must never be over-conscious, and that is where the skill lies. Finding the language in this way, the text becomes rooted in the whole body, and not just the emotion.

Speech Structures

This is one of the most useful areas to tackle at the beginning of any rehearsal period: I would say a key area, because it both informs the way the character thinks – their inner debate. It gives a structure to the text: and it is through that structure that the meaning, however complex, gets through to the audience. But more than that it asks the question of the actor: does the character know what they are going to say before they speak, or are they speaking in response to what has just been said to them, or to the situation and firming up their ideas as they go along? Obviously this will vary with the particular situation, but there will always be a discovery along the way.

In Shakespeare there is always a very clear format to any speech of length, or to any soliloquy. First, the character lays out the premise; that premise is then argued through; in the process the character goes to different parts of their mind – present circumstance, past experience or some personal attitude or philosophy – which may inform both the premise and the subsequent action; they will then reach some kind of conclusion, be it action or non-action.

On the way through there may be various rhetorical devices – antithesis, assonance, alliteration, etc – which point up the underlying state or mood, but I want to stress how important it is that that first thought or premise is given just a little more time so that it lays on the hearer's consciousness, and then you can run with the thoughts and develop them as quickly as you wish.

To reiterate: taking that split moment to lay the first thought does not slow the text up; rather, it helps to quicken it.

The most obvious example of this is Hamlet's 'To be, or not to be...', where he is debating the action of suicide, and in doing so, goes to many dark corners of his mind, and ends up with no conclusion having been made – no action. But the journey is there – the premise, laying out the possibilities, the philosophical debate and the possibility of a conclusion, broken only by the appearance of Ophelia.

The following speech from *Othello* is quite different: it has a female view of survival at the centre. Emilia is trying to comfort Desdemona who is distraught by Othello's apparent anger, the reason for which is unknown to her. In doing so, Emilia argues through her views regarding men and their attitudes to women. She lays out quite clearly at the beginning that any fault the woman may have is a direct result of the bad treatment she has received from the man.

EMILIA: But I do think it is their husband's faults
If wives do fall. Say that they slack their duties,
And pour our treasures into foreign laps;
Or else break out in peevish jealousies,
Throwing restraint upon us; or say they strike us,
Or scant our former having in despite –
Why, we have galls, and though we have some grace,
Yet have we some revenge. Let husbands know
Their wives have sense like them: they see and smell,
And have their palates both for sweet and sour
As husbands have. What is it that they do,
When they change us for others? Is it sport?
I think it is. And doth affection breed it?
I think it doth. Is't frailty that thus errs?

It is so too. And have not we affections,
Desires for sport, and frailty, as men have?
Then let them use us well: else let them know
The ills we do, their ills instruct us so.[1]

She states her case in the first line and a half, then with the experience of her life behind her, she argues through all her reasons and ends up with those last two lines which express her total disbelief in the honesty of men, and therefore her need to survive in her own way. But that first line and a half has to lay with the hearer, for it is at the centre of her thinking, and then as she gets carried away with her subject the thoughts quicken, and we can take them at speed.

To work on this the group would need to read it through as for the exercise on Egeus (page 52) – ie, to go to a different part of the space for each new thought. But here it is not simply about feeling how her thoughts move, but rather being aware of how she goes to a different part of herself for each new thought, each new idea. We are made aware of what she is finding within herself – dipping into her own experience, and how those ladders of thought lead her to her conclusion because each new thought takes her to a different place, so we hear how the cadence of the speech lifts us through and feeds our curiosity:

Then let them use us well: else let them know
The ills we do, their ills instruct us so.

This sense of structure works equally for modern text, be it Brecht, Osborne or Caryl Churchill.

When looking at speech structures we must always keep our minds open to antithesis within a speech, because it is through expressing the opposites that we are able somehow to quantify our own feelings.

A wonderful example of antithetical thinking is Juliet's speech, when she hears that Romeo has killed her cousin Tybalt. Her

1   *Othello*, IV iii.

feelings are so extreme that she can only express them through extremes of imagery:

JULIET: O serpent heart, hid with a flowering face!
Did ever dragon keep so fair a cave!
Beautiful tyrant! Fiend angelical!
Dove-feathered raven! Wolvish-ravening lamb!
Despisèd substance of divinest show!
Just opposite to what thou justly seemest –
A damnèd saint, an honourable villain!
O nature, what hadst thou to do in hell
When thou didst bower the spirit of a fiend
In mortal paradise of such sweet flesh?
Was ever book containing such vile matter
So fairly bound? O, that deceit should dwell
In such a gorgeous palace![1]

A really simple exercise to do on this is to mark out two squares in the space quite near to each other: one square is for the good image, one for the bad.

- The actor then needs to move to the appropriate square for the image being spoken.
- By going to these different spaces the images are separated and so become more surprising and extreme – and perhaps, as in Juliet's case – confused, so the actor experiences the confusion both in the body and the mind. (I cannot think of a modern example for this – perhaps it is all in the subtext.)

Where the Image Lies

I like to do an exercise, near the beginning of my work in any company, which focuses on imagery, and how imagery is not just an intellectual description of a feeling or an idea, but rather it is where the character is living within their body at that moment in time. It is a group exercise.

---

1 *Romeo and Juliet*, III ii.

We need, therefore, to get the actor to embrace the image as they speak it, let it into their bodies, and this is most effectively done by mime:

- The best way to do this is to get someone to read a speech out loud, a phrase at a time. As they do this the group should repeat the words, while at the same time miming the images that are there in the text they are speaking.

The most evocative example of this, and one which I often use because it gets the point over so clearly, is Juliet's speech in *Romeo and Juliet* (III ii), while she is waiting for Romeo to come. It is great because it is quite extreme, and so getting a group to gallop around as they repeat the phrases takes away all inhibitions, plus they begin to feel the extreme sensuality which is there in the speech –

JULIET: Gallop apace, you fiery-footed steeds,
Towards Phoebus' lodging! Such a waggoner
As Phaëton would whip you to the West
And bring in cloudy night immediately.
Spread thy close curtain, love-performing night,
That runaway's eyes may wink, and Romeo
Leap to these arms untalked of and unseen.
Lovers can see to do their amorous rites
By their own beauties; or if love be blind
It best agrees with night. Come, civil night,
Thou sober-suited matron, all in black,
And learn me how to lose a winning match,
Played for a pair of stainless maidenhoods.
Hood my unmanned blood, baiting in my cheeks,
With thy black mantle till strange love grow bold,
Think true love acted simple modesty.
Come, night. Come, Romeo. Come, thou day in night;
For thou wilt lie upon the wings of night
Whiter than new snow upon a raven's back.
Come, gentle night. Come, loving, black-browed nigh,
Give me my Romeo. And when I shall die,
Take him and cut him out in little stars,

> And he will make the face of heaven so fine
> That all the world will be in love with night
> And pay no worship to the garish sun.
> O I have bought the mansion of a love
> But not possessed it; and though I am sold,
> Not yet enjoyed. So tedious is this day
> As is the night before some festival
> To an impatient child that has new robes
> And may not wear them.

The images are truly amazing, and she finds them within herself with their mixture of sexuality and innocence –

> 'Sober-suited matron'
> 'Love-performing night'
> 'Hood my unmanned blood'
> 'Wings of night'
> 'Whiter than snow upon a raven's back'
> 'And when I shall die…'

– that last a euphemism for having an orgasm –

> 'Cut him out in little stars'
> 'Mansion of a love'

– and then to finish with an image of an impatient child –

> 'that hath new robes
> And may not wear them.'

Her blood is truly galloping.

You could also go through this speech of Portia in *The Merchant of Venice* in the same way – it is of course much more restrained in feeling than Juliet's, nor does it have the physicality of her language, plus it is an argument which she is presenting in a legal manner. However, to work it through miming as many of the images as possible will make one aware of where she is in her own mind and the resolve and precision of her reasoning.

It will not be as simple to mime as Juliet's speech because the thinking is quite metaphysical, but however you manage it each idea will become very clear and so take us into her private mind. It makes the thinking so specific.

PORTIA: The quality of mercy is not strained,
            It droppeth as the gentle rain from heaven
            Upon the place beneath. It is twice blest,
            It blesseth him that gives and him that takes.
            'Tis mightiest in the mightiest, it becomes
            The thronèd monarch better than his crown.
            His sceptre shows the force of temporal power,
            The attribute to awe and majesty,
            Wherein doth sit the dread and fear of kings;
            But mercy is above this sceptred sway,
            It is enthronèd in the hearts of kings,
            It is an attribute to God himself,
            And earthly power doth then show likest God's
            When mercy seasons justice. Therefore, Jew,
            Though justice be thy plea, consider this:
            That in the course of justice none of us
            Should see salvation. We do pray for mercy,
            And that same prayer doth teach us all to render
            The deeds of mercy. I have spoke thus much
            To mitigate the justice of thy plea,
            Which if thou follow, this strict court of Venice
            Must needs give sentence 'gainst the merchant there.[1]

There are just endless examples of speeches one could use – *Richard II* for instance when he says:

            Down, down I come like glistering Phaethon,
            Wanting the manage of unruly jades…[2]

We know, regardless of the irony, that that is his self-image, the image he lives with.

---

1   *The Merchant of Venice*, IV i.
2   *Richard II*, III iii.

Or as with Brutus, in his soliloquy when contemplating the murder of Caesar, he ends with the lines –

> And therefore think him as a serpent's egg,
> Which, hatched, would, as his kind, grow mischievous,
> And kill him in the shell.[1]

The image of the 'serpent's egg' takes us into that world of political subterfuge, and we know that he has persuaded himself of the rightness of his cause.

The Word Itself

Because, as I have already said, we live in such a literate and literal society, our main objective when we read a text is to make the meaning clear, so we tend to read everything in what I call clumps of sense. In doing this, we forget that each thought structure is made up of specific words, and sometimes it can be illuminating to break the logic of the phrasing in some way, either by repeating words at random or by going through a piece of text word by word. Here are three ideas.

ONE

- This exercise is done with the whole group speaking together: you need to take a piece of text and speak it through together once so you understand the sense of the whole – it can be a poem or a speech from a play.

- Now you need to speak it literally one word at a time, yet keeping the sense of the whole phrase.

- This takes quite a bit of concentration, for we are so used to reading a whole phrase at a time that our minds are on to the next word before we have finished the one we are speaking: each word has to be separate – yet connected in thought to the one before and the one after.

---

1 *Julius Caesar*, II 1 (see page 117).

- We have looked in detail both in the Workshop (page 38), and earlier in this section at the movement of thoughts – how one thought triggers off the next – in this exercise we hear how one word triggers off the next and lifts the language through in a surprising way.

Any of the texts we have looked at so far would yield much, eg, Leontes – 'Inch-thick, knee-deep...' (page 67).

- In this speech we found how each thought fed the next, and as the thoughts accumulated so the images he finds to express his feelings became wilder and more potent.

- But in this exercise we hear how one word triggers off the next and becomes almost too much to bear –

- It makes us notice how even the seemingly least significant words so often adds to the meaning of the whole.

In Ophelia's speech (quoted on page 61), for instance:

- If you take one word at a time you would hear right at the beginning that one word – 'what' – which is usually run over as part of the grammar of the sentence, but when it is isolated it actually carries with it the sense of 'to what extent', or 'almost beyond compare', and this adds to its collective meaning.

- You will notice many things as you go through it, eg, that word 'mind', with its image of the head and all the activity going on within it, becomes so specific to one's image of Hamlet – and therefore special.

- Then 'overthrown' – takes on quite a violent meaning.

- If you work through the whole speech in this way, hearing her very exact and personal description of him you will hear an extraordinary momentum which comes to its climax on that one word 'blasted' – and perhaps that is where her madness begins.

Another good speech to look at in this context is that of Claudio in *Measure for Measure* –

Ay, but to die, and go we know not where.
To lie in cold obstruction and to rot;
This sensible warm motion to become
A kneaded clod; and the delighted spirit
To bathe in fiery floods, or to reside
In thrilling region of thick-ribbed ice,
To be imprison'd in the viewless winds
And blown with restless violence round about
The pendent world; or to be worse than worst
Of those that lawless and incertain thought
Imagine howling, 'tis too horrible.
The weariest and most loathèd worldly life
That age, ache, penury, and imprisonment
Can lay on nature is a paradise
To what we fear of death.[1]

- To get the full horror of his thoughts we need at some moment
  to experience each word individually. If you take this through
  one word at a time and hear where his imagination takes him,
  the horror becomes overwhelming, and is summed up in those
  last four lines.

You could also work it on something less emotive such as the
Chorus to Act IV of *Henry V*. It is a description of the two camps,
French and English, the night before Agincourt. It is quite a familiar
speech, but if you take it word for word you hear how each word is
filled with quite sensuous images –

'creeping murmur...'
'wide vessel of the universe...'
'through the foul womb of night...' etc.

Or you could do it on a poem, such as the following Hopkins sonnet:

---

1 *Measure for Measure*, III i.

Spring

Nothing is so beautiful as Spring –
When weeds, in wheels, shoot long and lovely and
  lush;
Thrush's eggs look little low heavens, and thrush
Through the echoing timber does so rinse and wring
The ear, it strikes like lightnings to hear him sing.
The glassy peartree leaves and blooms, they brush
The descending blue; that blue is all in a rush
With richness; the racing lambs too have fair their fling.

What is all this juice and all this joy?
A strain of the earth's sweet being in the beginning
In Eden garden. – Have, get, before it cloy,

Before it cloud, Christ, lord, and sour with sinning,
Innocent mind and Mayday in girl and boy,
Most, O maid's child, thy choice and worthy the
  winning.[1]

This may seem a rather simplistic exercise, but the point I want to get over is that, because we read things in clumps of sense, we miss the resonance of a word and its specific meaning. This poem is so full of dense images that can so easily get lost in a wash of generalised beauty.

The exercise probably does not work so well for humour because, as I have already said, humour is so deeply embedded in the rhythm. Even so, it will make one hear it in a different way, and that is always worth the time.

TWO
This second exercise makes us aware of language in a different way, and again it can be done on a speech from the text which is in rehearsal.

---

1 Gerard Manley Hopkins, 'Spring'.

- As you work through a speech you repeat at random one word in each line – by 'at random' I mean that the word does not necessarily have a particular depth of meaning, it is simply a word that you fancy at the moment of speaking. But it needs to be repeated two or three times.

- It can be done either singly or with a group.

- Now because this obviously interrupts the literal meaning of the whole phrase, it allows that word to go deeper into your subconscious response and so allows another layer of under-standing into it. Because it has interrupted your natural rhythm of thought – so ruled by grammatical sense – it makes you think the meaning afresh, and therefore surprises. It can also be done as a group exercise, walking round the space – it is a little chaotic but good all the same.

THREE

Finally, I always remember an exercise that Peter Brook used to do: he would take a short piece of text with which the group is familiar, it could be –

To be, or not to be, that is the question…

and get them to speak that text round in the circle one word at a time.

- The phrase should be comprised of a few words more than the number in the group so that each time they go round they will start at a different place and get a different word.

- They may find it difficult to begin with and perhaps it will sound rather broken up, but the aim is that in the end it will sound as one smooth phrase with each person being specific to their word, yet being an integral part of the whole thought.

- It is good because although the phrase becomes familiar, we begin to hear the many choices within it and, most important, it makes us part of the same world.

To sum up

All this is work that can, and should, be done at different times throughout the rehearsal period to keep us alive to the word itself, so we stay tuned in to the language of the play, and how that language is forever shifting. The choice of exercise will of course depend on the play and on where you are in rehearsal, and they can be bent in any way that serves the work best – they are quite closely linked anyway. The bottom line is that they put the text at the centre of the imaginative process.

Chapter Five

DISPLACEMENT STRATEGIES

THE STRATEGIES OR EXERCISES which I am now going to lay out are, for me, at the centre of my work on text. In rehearsal the focus for both the actor and the director has to be on opening out the world of the play, and the motives and feelings which are driving both the story and the characters. To do this we have to look in detail at the text, for we know that the answers to all our questions lie there. We also know that it will never come to life until we speak it aloud: but how do we really hear what is there in the text without colouring it with our own assumptions and values and meanings? That is surely the bottom-line question: reading a text and hearing it are two totally different experiences.

So the reasons for the strategies are as follows – they are about:

i Uncovering the sound and language beneath the surface and so finding that other world within the character and within the actor.

ii The actor being behind what they are saying without thinking about how they are saying it.

iii The surprise, the anarchy, in the language.

iv Realising that language springs from the body as well as the mind.

In other words, they are about allowing one's subliminal connection to the words enrich the speaking of them.

As we get into rehearsal the questions about the strategies will always be 'When and where and what'; and these are not so easy to pin down, for the choice of exercise is never simple.

At the beginning you have to take chances and experiment, but once you have used an exercise its benefit will become apparent. Also the actors have to trust the strategies, and this will not happen until they have experienced how it helps them connect with their own instinctive responses. The extraordinary thing is that, because the work has evolved out of the very form and sound of the language rather than its specific and literal meaning, the strategies can be used for both serious and comic writing alike, for they will always bring out the underlying nuances.

I felt I needed to name them in order to clarify their purpose both for myself and for others, so I started by calling them 'Diversion' strategies, but somehow that did not seem pro-active enough. Then the word 'Displacement' came into my head, so I looked it up in the dictionary and part of the definition for 'displacement' was –

> The act or an instance of displacing: the process of an instance of being displaced.

But then, to my surprise, the next definition in the dictionary was – 'displacement activity' – and against that it said the following –

> Animal, or human activity which seems irrelevant to the situation.

and that seemed to me to hit it exactly right, for the exercises are irrelevant to the situation, yet become part of it. It did go on to add an example –

> eg, Head-scratching (when confused)

– however that is a strategy I do not use!

I think the exercises fall roughly into two areas.

i The first is to do with finding one's private, and therefore perhaps deeper, response to the language.

ii The second is how, by some sort of physical resistance or aggressive act, we find the roughness in the language and perhaps its unexpectedness, and the response to it through our own body.

As I have said, the strategies all involve some kind of displacement activity or resistance, some of which we worked through in the Workshop sessions on pages 41 and 56, and they can be used for both solo and scene work.

For the director, although you are not speaking the text through yourself, because you are hearing it in a new and unplanned way, this work can often throw up other possibilities and ways of doing a scene. Also, because the actor is freed from the straightjacket of 'making sense' of the situation, they perhaps feel a greater freedom to experiment, and this can also give a new and interesting focus to the work.

I have not set the work down in any specific order because each exercise has its own usefulness, so to begin with the choice of strategy or exercise may seem problematic, but once you have tried a few of them the underlying reasons become apparent. If one exercise is not helping, it will usually tell you which other one to try. The important thing is that once you catch on to the basic reasons behind the work, you can be as imaginative as you like, and alter an exercise to suit the particular requirements of the scene you are working on.

As we well know the actor has to work on many skills in order that their performance, whether it be in theatre, film or television, will reach the audience in as complete a way as possible: skills relating to vocal tone and clarity, to the movement and rhythm of the text, to the imagery in the language. All this is essential, but when this is done she or he has to make that language their own, it has to be rooted in the whole of themselves – in the body as well as the mind. So the benefit of this work lies in the fact that because part of their mind is on another activity, or involved in another purpose, they are freed from the responsibility of speaking the text how they think it should be spoken, and making it clear; this then allows other possibilities to emerge which can both enlighten and free the imagination. The activity has to be one which can be done fairly automatically, and without too much creative thought.

I will be working many of the texts that I used in *Text in Action* for the exercises, partly because they are pieces that illustrate the work in a particularly clear way; but also because I think it is useful to see how a text can be continually opened up and developed in different ways, both for the director and for the actor. And as I have already said the texts, with one or two exceptions, will be from Shakespeare, because they illustrate the work so clearly and simply, and also because of the general familiarity with his work. But I do stress that the exercises are equally useful for all texts of whatever period: the choice is simply to do with linking the strategy to the situation in the play.

Now for the strategies…

Performing a Task

This first exercise takes no time to set up. It may seem simple but it so often throws up other nuances and inflections which are there in the text which we do not necessarily hear when focusing on the logic. It can be used for both solo work and dialogue, plus it can be used at different stages of rehearsal.

It is basically about giving the actor or actors a task while working through a scene or a speech – a task which requires a certain specificity but little reasoned thought.

- If working on a scene with two or more actors, you could ask them to rearrange the chairs in the room in a particular order.

- Or you could throw a lot of articles – ie, books, bags, etc – into the middle of the space and get the group to clear everything up.

- If the work is solo, the activity should be more detailed – for instance folding a piece of paper in a very precise shape, or copying some writing onto a piece of paper. The choice of activity will depend upon what there is to use in the space, and here your imagination comes into play.

- However, it is always useful to ensure that there are enough objects about which can be used when needed – usually there are plenty of boxes around which are available. In addition, a pack of cards is always a useful prop to have about you, as it can be used in so many different ways: you can ask the actor or actors to put them in a specific order, or deal them out, or even play a game of patience.

- Whatever you choose, it needs to be something which is simple but precise – it could even be a bag of potatoes thrown on the floor which have to be picked up and put back into the bag.

The point is that, while the actor knows exactly what they want to convey, the very act of performing a task while speaking the text stops them 'over-controlling' – ie, ensuring that everything is made clear – and so releases a different energy in the language, and a different phrasing. The great thing is that it can be used for any scene, or part of a scene at any time; whether the prevailing mood is angry, conciliatory or plain matter-of-fact, it will nearly always surprise. But most important, it will make us aware that perhaps we do not have to underline the meaning so much, but rather let our basic understanding of the text have its own space and time. This strategy is particularly useful near the end of a rehearsal period when ideas and motives are beginning to get fixed – this stirs them up.

Resistance

Resistance exercises are always about putting something in the way of the actor which makes it difficult for her/him to move freely, and therefore to speak: now the actor of course knows that it is a game which has been set up, yet one's primal urge to protect and assert oneself comes into play and so he/she instinctively fights back and this energy is reflected in the words: as in any game, we do not like to lose.

Resistance exercises can take a number of forms, some quite mild and some more aggressive, but they all make us realise that the act of speaking is never passive.

- If the actor is working a speech which is about extremes of feeling, get the group to surround them in a fairly close circle. The aim of the actor is then to get out of the circle and cross to the other side of the space while speaking the text. This was very clearly described in the Introductory Workshop (page 64), on the speech of Leontes. In that exercise the group surrounds the actor playing Leontes so that the more he tries to get out of the circle the more the words take over and he uses them to push through the circle. We hear how this physical need to speak feeds the jealousy he feels inside, and conversely, how that jealousy feeds the sexual disgust in the language.

- What is wonderful is that the listener hears the deep anger and frustration which is there both in the discovery of the words, and in their sound – the language is there in the body as well as the mind.

- But what is also good is that we hear how he is thinking – the frustration is feeding his inner debate, and his need to convey that debate.

- Watch that the exercise does not get too rough or the scene itself will get lost.

- If you are working on dialogue, you can get two or three members of the group to stand behind each of the characters and hold them back as they try to reach each other.

- This can also get quite rough and so release extreme feelings into the language: at a less extreme level this resistance can be varied by getting the group to keep the characters involved in the scene away from each other simply by walking around and occupying the space between them – so keeping them apart. This should be done not by physically holding on to them in any way, but simply by making it difficult for them to get together.

- This is a gentler version which might be more appropriate for the scene in hand.

- Also you can get the group to form some sort of obstruction with chairs, etc, so they cannot reach each other easily – there are many possibilities according to the space you are in.

- The point is that anything which makes it difficult for the two characters to reach each other with the language, increases their desire to do just that, be it because of anger, or because of pain, or because of love, and this is unconsciously reflected in their response to the language itself – ie, the length of the vowels and the vibration and muscularity of the consonants.

I did a production of *Hamlet* back in 1985 for the National Theatre Studio, and I remember how, while rehearsing the scene between Hamlet and his mother, the group kept them apart by building an obstruction between them so that they could not reach each other – and how it quite unconsciously released both Hamlet's and Gertrude's pain, and also their anger. And that is the point, it does not only release the aggression in the language, but also the pain or the longing. You will have felt how the words have inhabited your body, and how the sounds carry the depth of thought, which in turn carries the feeling, so that when you come back to speaking it normally, in situ that is, that awareness will stay with you and the language will keep its full resonance of meaning. One thinks of Nina in *The Seagull* trying to reach out to Konstantin.

This work on resistance in some form is probably at the base of all the work, for it makes us realise that any form of communication, however off-beat or minimal, is a way of reaching out to some other person and affirming one's presence in some way – and yet you can be 'cool' at the same time: but most important, it makes us realise that words always cost something.

Repeating words

This is a different kind of exercise altogether, it is simply about listening and responding. I say 'simply about listening and responding', but in fact, as we all know, that is not as easy as it seems. While rehearsing, the actor is learning about their own character, they are thinking about their relationship with the other characters, about the overall meaning, and how to move the story on: the result is that it is easy to get into patterns, and to be just a little too ready. It is therefore extremely useful, at different stages in rehearsal, to take a little time to remind ourselves of the words being used and what they convey.

In the first exercise in the introductory workshop we looked at how the specific vocabulary takes us into the world of the play, but of course it also takes us into the world of the character. So when rehearsing a scene it can be very refreshing to repeat words at random that another character is speaking: I say refreshing, because it so often opens our ears to the subtextual resonances of the language and again awakens our responses – it makes us hear differently.

If, for instance you were working on the second scene of *The Winter's Tale*, and you asked Leontes to repeat all the words with sexual implications in the following speech of Hermione, you would hear a whole private world there which is presumably shared between them, and we recognise immediately why his jealousy has such a fierce hold on him – their world is a sensual one. At Leontes' request, Hermione has managed to persuade their guest Polixines to stay longer:

LEONTES: At my request he would not.
          Hermione, my dearest, thou never spok'st
          To better purpose.
HERMIONE: Never?
LEONTES: Never but once.
HERMIONE: What? Have I twice said well? When was't before?
          I prithee tell me. Cram's with praise, and make's
          As fat as tame things. One good deed dying tongueless
          Slaughters a thousand waiting upon that.
          Our praises are our wages.[1]

---

1 *The Winter's Tale*, I ii.

The language is both sensual in sound as well as in meaning.

So she continues with – 'You may ride's with one soft kiss...', etc: if, as Leontes listens to her, he repeats those words which have sexual undertones, the more this will feed his unfounded jealousy.

In dialogue the key strategy for me however, is the following:

- When you have worked on a scene for a bit, and the actors are reasonably sure of where they want to take it, go through it again but this time ask each actor to repeat the last word spoken to they before they reply.

- It is important that the actor allows that word to drop in and so impel their response.

- This can so often be wonderfully surprising and take the actor off in a new direction, and thus give the scene a whole new energy: it is surprising because we cannot pre-think our answer – we are taken off guard and have to reply to the specific word spoken.

Say this is done with the early dialogue between Hermia and Lysander in the *Dream*:

- We hear how they are vying with each other for the most dramatic and evocative way to describe both their love and the danger of their situation.

- As they repeat the last word that the other is saying, we hear how quickly they pick up on each other's thoughts, and imme-diately take them further – and end up planning their escape. It begins:

LYSANDER: How now, my love? Why is your cheek so pale?
How come the roses there do fade so fast?

HERMIA: Belike for want of rain, which I could well
Beteem them from the tempest of my eyes.

LYSANDER: Ay, me! For aught that I could ever read,
Could ever hear by tale or history,
The course of true love never did run smooth;
But either it was different in blood –

HERMIA:	O cross! – too high to be enthralled to low.
LYSANDER:	Or else misgraffèd in respect of years –
HERMIA:	O spite! – too old to be engaged to young.
LYSANDER:	Or else it stood upon the choice of friends –
HERMIA:	O hell! – to choose love by another's eyes
LYSANDER:	Or if there were a sympathy in choice...[1]

and so the scene continues – it is as if they are breathing together. If you go through it just repeating those end words, you hear how they each fly with the other's thoughts, and it gives it so much life.

In a totally different mood and style, you can try the same strategy on the scene between Bushy, Bagot and Green in *Richard II* (II ii). As they begin to realise the likelihood of Richard being deposed by Bolingbroke, and the consequent danger to them, they are each deciding what best to do in this changing political world.

BUSHY:	The wind sits fair for news to go for Ireland,
	But none returns. For us to levy power
	Proportionable to the enemy
	Is all impossible.
GREEN:	Besides, our nearness to the King in love
	Is near the hate of those love not the King.
BAGOT:	And that is the wavering commons; for their love
	Lies in their purses, and whoso empties them
	By so much fills their hearts with deadly hate.
BUSHY:	Wherein the King stands generally condemn'd.
BAGOT:	If judgement lie in them, then so do we,
	Because we ever have been near the King.
GREEN:	Well, I will for refuge straight to Bristol Castle,
	The Earl of Wiltshire is already there.
BUSHY:	Thither will I with you; for little office
	Will the hateful commons perform for us –
	Except like curs to tear us all to pieces.
	Will you go along with us?
BAGOT:	No, I will to Ireland to his majesty.

---

1   *A Midsummer Night's Dream*, I i.

	Farewell. If heart's presages be not vain,
	We three here part that ne'er shall meet again.
GREEN:	Alas, poor Duke! The task he undertakes
	Is numbering sands and drinking oceans dry,
	Where one on his side fights, thousands will fly.
BAGOT:	Farewell at once, for once, for all, and ever.
BUSHY:	Well, we may meet again.
BAGOT:	I fear me, never.

As this piece of text is a good deal more thoughtful, it would be best to repeat the last two or three words of each line so that the complexity of the situation is allowed to drop in. You will then hear how their thinking is continually shifting, each feeding the other's fears, and how finally their will to survive takes over with the sense of fate in that final couplet –

BAGOT:	Farewell at once, for once, for all, and ever/
BUSHY:	Well, we may meet again.
BAGOT:	I fear me never.

It is a wonderful balancing act.

Spaces of the Mind

For me this is one of the most interesting and telling strategies. First, it clarifies the structure of a speech, be it classical or modern, and in so doing helps the actor discover the processes of thought within a character, the debate, and how one thought kicks off the next. It also allows us to recognise the different places of the mind from which those thoughts are springing – plus the different impulses feeding them: each thought has a different impulse, and this gives it a different texture. And because the actor is moving to a different part of the space, their voice unconsciously responds to the changes, and so we get the varying tones of those thoughts – their different resonances.

As we saw when we looked at speech structures in the last chapter, a speech starts by stating the general premise, ie, the main trend of thought. The character then argues that idea through until they come to some conclusion, but in the process of arguing it through the character goes to so many places in their head, or in their experience, and that is what makes it interesting. In this exercise the actor needs to think of the rehearsal space as the space in their head, and so go to a different place in that space for each specific thought.

- She or he needs to go to a spot in the rehearsal room where they feel comfortable, and speak the first thought – this can be to the first full-stop, or simply to a turn in the thought.

- At that point they must go to another part of the space and speak the next thought – but they must not speak while moving.

- It can often be quite good to crouch while they are speaking – but not necessary.

- Let them do what feels comfortable: they should move at the speed of their thinking.

I think the benefit is felt immediately for, by going to a different place for each specific thought, that thought is not only clarified but becomes integral to the experience of the character, and so enriches the actor's whole concept of that character. It allows the actor to sit in each thought and inhabit it before moving on. It is very much to do with how we think in ordinary life, we are always moving to different parts of our brain, of our experience and our intuition, as we think through a moment of change. The thoughts in themselves become actions, one thought impelling the next – and this awakens the listener's curiosity. But also the exercise allows the actor to sit in and occupy each thought as it happens, and not go on to the next before the one thought has impinged truly on the mind: it is being 'on' the thought, 'on' the word – and that is never easy.

It is a great exercise to do on any soliloquy, eg, Brutus in *Julius Caesar*, II i:

BRUTUS: It must be by his death; and for my part,
I know no personal cause to spurn at him,
But for the general. – He would be crowned.

116

How that might change his nature, there's the
  question.
It Is the bright day that brings forth the adder,
And that craves wary walking. Crown him! – that!
And then, I grant, we put a sting in him
That at his will he may do danger with.
Th'abuse of greatness is when it disjoins
Remorse from power; and, to speak truth of Caesar,
I have not known when his affections swayed
More than his reason. But 'tis a common proof,
That lowliness is young ambition's ladder,
Whereto the climber-upward turns his face;
But when he once attains the upmost round,
He then unto the ladder turns his back,
Looks in the clouds, scorning the base degrees
By which he did ascend: so Caesar may;
Then lest he may, prevent. And, since the quarrel
Will bear no quarrel for the thing he is,
Fashion it thus: that what he is, augmented,
Would run to these and these extremities;
And therefore think him as a serpent's egg
Which, hatched, would, as his kind, grow mischievous,
And kill him in the shell.[1]

This is such an interesting speech to look at because we never really know whether that first thought is a statement or a question: in other words, has he made up his mind right at the beginning that Caesar must be killed and so, by talking through his thoughts, he vindicates his decision? Or is it a genuine question which he then argues through and in the end decides, with reason, that Caesar must be killed – 'kill him in the shell'? He is debating with his conscience, and to do this he has to go to different areas of his own experience – his personal and his political self – and his knowledge of the world. His use of the image of the adder shows us where he is living in himself – in a world that cannot be trusted.

---

1 *Julius Caesar,* II i.

Once the actor has experienced the thoughts in this way, they can then go as quickly as they like, but that specificity will remain with them. We think to survive – so we have to think with speed. The important thing with any speech is that the first thought has its right space in order that the actor can take off with it, and so the listener is right there with the character. What is good about this exercise is that it defines the structure of a speech: this is very necessary if it is a long one, such as the speeches in *Coriolanus* – either of Coriolanus himself or of his mother Volumnia.

'Inner vs Outer Landscape' – In and Out of the Present

This in its way is similar to the last exercise in that it highlights how our past experience, or our philosophical outlook, influences the way we think and make decisions. Again it is particularly useful in discovering the structure of a speech, and how the thoughts are always shifting from one place to another, or one time to another, in the character's mind and are active in their outcome.

- First mark out a small space and divide it into two.
- The actor needs to be in one part of that space when he or she is speaking about what is happening now, in the present, and then move to the other part when speaking the inner thoughts of their mind.

These inner thoughts are to do with remembering something, or making some sort of judgement on the situation, moral or otherwise, which is prompted by their past experience. I think this happens a lot in our own lives: how our past experiences informs our present actions and our thinking.

A good example of this are the speeches of Brutus' wife Portia in *Julius Caesar* (II i), when she is pleading with her husband to tell her what is troubling him. The text is very powerful, for she knows that there is real danger brewing, and as she pleads with Brutus to tell her his thoughts, she goes to different parts of herself and her life. Here is part of it –

PORTIA: I charm you, by my once commended beauty

By all your vows of love, and that great vow
Which did incorporate and make us one,
That you unfold to me, your self, your half,
Why you are heavy, and what men tonight
Have had resort to you; for here have been
Some six or seven, who did hide their faces
Even from darkness.

BRUTUS: Kneel not, gentle Portia.

PORTIA: I should not need if you were gentle Brutus.
Within the bond of marriage, tell me, Brutus,
Is it excepted I should know no secrets
That appertain to you? Am I your self
But, as it were, in sort or limitation,
To keep with you at meals, comfort your bed,
And talk to you sometimes? Dwell I but in the suburbs
Of your good pleasure? If it be no more,
Portia is Brutus' harlot, not his wife.

BRUTUS: You are my true and honourable wife,
As dear to me as are the ruddy drops
That visit my sad heart.

PORTIA: If this were true, then should I know this secret.
I grant I am a woman; but withal
A woman that Lord Brutus took to wife;
I grant I am a woman; but withal
A woman well reputed, Cato's daughter.
Think you I am no stronger than my sex
Being so father'd and so husbanded?

It is a complex speech during which Portia goes to different parts
of her life's experience as she pleads with Brutus to tell her what
is happening, until she finally drops the bombshell of what she has
just done – what is there in this present moment of her life –

I have made strong proof of my constancy
Giving myself a voluntary wound
Here, in the thigh; can I bear that with patience,
And not my husband's secrets?

119

So many of the speeches in classical writing, particularly Shakespeare's, have this specific interchange of what I call the inner and outer landscape of a person's thoughts, and this exercise of going between two spaces helps to clarify these two areas of the mind for the actor, and how the character is challenged by them. This in turn actively involves the listener in the debate, because it keeps taking us to different places and so continually excites our curiosity – the thoughts are always active. I think in modern text it is more subtle, for the past is always informing the present in the subtext: yet the exercise can still be done so we hear what is predominant.

Drawing a Picture

This is a strategy which I find particularly useful: by asking the actor to draw something on a piece of paper while speaking the text they connect with that text in a very particular way, and this is intriguing for the listener because we perceive that the actor is both visualising and finding their thoughts as they speak – we hear the detail. Because they are having to be as precise as possible about their drawing, it makes them also precise in finding the words they need in order to express their thoughts accurately.

For the exercise the actor needs to draw a scene or an object on a piece of paper, the choice of subject for the drawing is dependent on what is needed both from the actor, and from the situation.

- If perhaps what is needed is a certain objectivity, then ask the actor to draw what they can see on the other side of the room as accurately as possible, or what they can see out of the window: it could be something moving, traffic for instance, or it could be quite still.

- However if it is a more reclusive speech, dealing with some difficulty within the character or situation, it can be very helpful to ask the actor to draw something within their own memory – eg, the street they live on, or their bedroom

- Or you could ask them to draw the first house they lived in, for this would allow them to touch base with their memory without getting emotional or psychological about it; they keep a certain distance.

- What is important is that it somehow allows them to feed their own personal resonances into the language, and in doing so the language becomes very real and rooted, giving it a certain depth.

- It is an exercise which is particularly effective when working on a soliloquy, where the character is discovering their inner feelings and motives – those of Ophelia (page 61) or Isabella (see below, page 123) would be clear choices.

- The speech of Claudio from *Measure for Measure*, III i, which we looked at in the last chapter (page 101), would also be excellent.

- It would be interesting to ask the actor to draw something beautiful that they remember, for this would be the antithesis of the images in the speech, and so would feed Claudio's need to get through to Isabella.

However in a different way it can be very helpful in a scene with two or more characters, each thinking out a common problem, but from separate points of view: this would underline the distance between them.

For instance it would work well in the scene between Goneril and Regan at the end of the first scene of *King Lear*. The conversation happens at the end of a momentous scene with Lear and his retinue and family: momentous in both the change of hierarchy that occurs, for Lear has disposed of his lands, and in family alignments, for he has banished Cordelia. The two sisters are left together contemplating how they are going to handle the future, and their father, with all that that entails.

- They are each off in their own world, thinking what is going to be best for them.

- As they exchange their thoughts, ask them each to draw what they can see out of the window.

- This sense of distance will feed their enquiry about the future, plus give them a certain objectivity and separateness which can be very powerful to watch – they are each in their own world, looking after their own interests.

GONERIL: Sister, it is not little I have to say of what most nearly appertains to us both. I think our father will hence tonight.

REGAN: That's most certain, and with you; next month with us.

GONERIL: You see how full of changes his age is. The observation we have made of it hath been but little. He always loved our sister most; and with what poor judgement he hath now cast her off appears too grossly.

REGAN: 'Tis the infirmity of his age. Yet he hath ever but slenderly known himself.

GONERIL: The best and soundest of his time hath been but rash. Then must we look from his age to receive not alone the imperfections of long-ingraffed condition, but therewithal the unruly waywardness that infirm and choleric years bring with them.

REGAN: Such unconstant starts are we like to have from him as this of Kent's banishment.

GONERIL: There is further compliment of leave-taking between France and him. Pray you, let us hit together. If our father carry authority with such disposition as he bears, this last surrender of his will but offend us.

REGAN: We shall further think of it.

GONERIL: We must do something, and i'th'heat.

This exercise works so well between people who are not quite connecting, yet at the same time are reliant on each other.

Concretising Thought

This ploy is good when a character is arguing through a set of complex ideas with themselves, or with another character. if working on a solo speech, get the actor to choose a small object such as a cup, or a small bottle, or a pen, and place it on a table in front of them.

- The item, though small, is solid in form and is there to represent the centre thought or idea in a speech.
- That centre idea is then linked to a concrete form, it has its own gravitas, and so becomes more real to the speaker, and somehow of more import and specificity. As the actor works through the speech ask them to move the object to another part of the table for each new turn of the thought.
- It is particularly interesting in that it both clarifies the ideas and makes the thinking active and progressive.
- An interesting speech on which to try it out would be Isabella from *Measure for Measure* (II iv): she has just been importuned by Angelo to give up her body to him in exchange for her brother's life – her brother having been sentenced to death for getting his lady Juliet with child.
- The central issue is her chastity, and Isabella has to work out which is more important – her purity or Claudio's life. The object represents her chastity.

ISABELLA: To whom should I complain? Did I tell this,
Who would believe me? O perilous mouths,
That bear in them one and the selfsame tongue,
Either of condemnation or approof,
Bidding the law make curtsy to their will,
Hooking both right and wrong to th'appetite,
To follow as it draws. I'll to my brother,
Though he hath fall'n by prompture of the blood,
Yet hath he in him such a mind of honour
That, had he twenty heads to tender down
On twenty bloody blocks, he'd yield them up,
Before his sister should her body stoop
To such abhorred pollution.
Then, Isabel, live chaste, and, brother die.
More than our brother is our chastity.

I'll tell him yet of Angelo's request,
And fit his mind to death, for his soul's rest.

If working in dialogue, it can also be very enlivening because, as each character takes hold of the thought and starts to wrestle with it, so they take hold of the object itself and move it to somewhere else on the table.

- This not only concretises that central idea and makes it tangible, it also gives the speaker that sense of owning the argument.

- Moving the object in this way makes the debate active in a positive way, and possibly competitive, thus giving it real significance.

There is a very sensitive exchange in *Richard II*, between Queen Isabel and Bushy: it starts the scene which we looked at earlier between Bushy, Bagot and Green (page 114), where we learn that the King is planning to embark for Ireland, and it begins with Bushy saying –

Madam, your majesty is too much sad...

and in his effort to comfort her the scene evolves into a metaphysical discussion about the substance of grief itself, which is quite involved, but also very moving:

BUSHY:	Madam, your majesty is too much sad.
	You promised, when you parted from the King
	To lay aside life-harming heaviness,
	And entertain a cheerful disposition.
Q ISABEL:	To please the King I did. To please myself
	I cannot do it. Yet I know no cause
	Why I should welcome such a guest as grief
	Save bidding farewell to so sweet a guest
	As my sweet Richard. Yet again methinks
	Some unborn sorrow ripe in fortune's womb
	Is coming towards me, and my inward soul
	With nothing trembles. At something it grieves
	More than with parting from my lord the King.

BUSHY: Each substance of a grief hath twenty shadows
Which shows like grief itself, but is not so.
For sorrow's eye, glazed with blinding tears,
Divides one thing entire to many objects
Like perspectives which, rightly gazed upon.
Show nothing but confusion, eyed awry,
Distinguish form. So your sweet majesty,
Looking awry upon your lord's departure,
Find shapes of grief more than himself to wail,
Which looked on as it is, is naught but shadows
Of what is not. Then, thrice-gracious Queen,
More than your lord's departure weep not – more is
  not seen,
Or if it be, 'tis with false sorrow's eye,
Which for things true weeps things imaginary.

Q ISABEL: It may be so; but yet my inward soul
Persuades me it is otherwise. Howe'er it be
I cannot but be sad – so heavy-sad
As, though on thinking on no thought I think,
Make me with heavy nothing faint and shrink.

BUSHY: 'Tis nothing but conceit, my gracious lady.

Q ISABEL: 'Tis nothing less. Conceit is still derived
From some forefather grief. Mine is not so,
For nothing hath begot my something grief,
Or something hath the nothing that I grieve –
'Tis in reversion that I do possess –
But what it is that is not yet known what,
I cannot name; 'tis nameless woe, I wot.[1]

Such complex thinking; yet if an object is used to represent grief as you work through the scene, the thoughts become specific in a very poignant, but unsentimental way.

---

1 *Richard II*, II ii.

- The exercise can be used in different ways to relate to the under-lying needs in a scene – perhaps by moving the object around the whole acting area, which could be both freeing for the actors, and also make the exchange perhaps more radical and confrontational.
- And of course the object can represent many different things: love, honour, friendship – and even perhaps absurdity.

Marking Thoughts

This is an exercise for a single actor, and is a quick but effective way of putting one in touch with the dynamic within the argument of a speech.

- It can be done either sitting or standing or walking about; put a piece of paper and a pencil on a chair or a table in the middle of the space you are working in.
- Then get the actor to speak the text and to put a tick on the paper at the end of each thought that they speak – it can be a whole thought or a part of a thought. You could work this on any of the texts we have looked at so far – the speech of Camillo would be particularly interesting – or, if something new, perhaps Enobarbus as he pictures Cleopatra in her barge.

When learning a speech the actor will focus on the main arc of the argument in hand, but this exercise throws up the twists of thought within that main argument, so that the text is forever active and engaging the curiosity of the audience as to how the matter will be resolved. It can often be quite surprising, and I like to think that there is never a full stop in a play until you come to its end.

One-Upmanship

This is a strategy on exactly the same lines as the previous one, but it is between two or more people. As before, put a piece of paper and a pencil on a chair or table in the middle of the space: now draw columns on the paper – one for each character – and as each character makes a point, so they must put a tick in the appropriate column. It is most useful when working on a debate where there is a lot at stake – eg, the big scene between Cassius and Brutus in *Julius Caesar*, I ii.

The ideal scene to illustrate this exercise is, of course, that between Katherine and Petruchio in *The Taming of the Shrew*, II i, where they each try to outwit the other.

The exercise not only clarifies the thoughts, but it also gives them an edge, for there is always that underlying insinuation that each character needs to make the best point – it makes it competitive: and actually that is a very human position. It highlights the issues between the characters, yet it does not necessarily have to be confrontational: it can be evocative if it is a dialogue between two lovers for instance, each trying to outdo the other in professing their love, be it Kate and Petruchio, Romeo and Juliet or Antony and Cleopatra. The great thing about it is that it will always bring out the humour which, if you are working on Shakespeare, is always hiding somewhere in the background.

Building Structures

This strategy has a wonderfully releasing effect, and again can be done both as solo work or in a scene. If the work is solo, ask the actor to build a structure, with whatever is in the room, to the central theme or motive of the speech they are working on – to its underlying purpose – it may be love, it may be revenge – whatever.

- First the actor has to imagine some sort of structure to fit their concept of that underlying motive.
- They will then have to find objects which they can use to construct that image – and so proceed to build as they speak.
- I always find it particularly rewarding, for just as the actor has to use their imagination to find an object in the room which can be part of that structure, so it subconsciously makes them find the word, the thought, in a new way.

Also because they are handling objects while speaking, the words become more tactile and expressive, both gentle and rough, and so the language itself becomes more 'found' and interesting. This speech of Berowne from *Love's Labours Lost* (IV iii), would yield so much, for the images are so specific, yet delicate, all describing the feeling of love.

BEROWNE: But love, first learnèd in a lady's eyes,
Lives not alone immurèd in the brain,
But with the motion of all elements
Courses as swift as thought in every power,
And gives to every power a double power,
Above their functions and their offices.
It adds a precious seeing to the eye:
A lover's eye will gaze an eagle blind.
A lover's ear will hear the lowest sound
When the suspicious head of theft is stopp'd.
Love's feeling is more soft and sensible
Than are the tender horns of cockled snails.
Love's tongue proves dainty Bacchus gross in taste.
For valour, is not Love a Hercules,
Still climbing trees in the Hesperides?
Subtle as Sphinx; as sweet and musical
As bright Apollo's lute, strung with his hair.
And when Love speaks, the voice of all the gods
Make heaven drowsy with the harmony.
Never durst poet touch a pen to write
Until his ink were tempered with Love's sighs.
O, then his lines would ravish savage ears
And plant in tyrants mild humility.
From women's eyes this doctrine I derive:
They sparkle still the right Promethean fire;
They are the books, the arts, the academs,
That show, contain, and nourish all the world;
Else none at all in aught proves excellent.
Then fools you were these women to forswear,
Or, keeping what is sworn, you will prove fools.
For wisdom's sake, a word that all men love,

> Or for love's sake, a word that loves all men,
> Or for men's sake, the authors of these women,
> Or women's sake, but whom we men are men –
> Let us once lose our oaths to find ourselves,
> Or else we lose ourselves to find our oaths.
> It is religion to be thus forsworn,
> For charity itself fulfils the law
> And who can sever love from charity?

How do you make a structure to fulfil these images –

> A lover's eyes will gaze an eagle blind...

or –

> Love's feeling is more soft and sensible
> Than are the tender horns of cockled snails... –

or –

> For valour is not love a Hercules,
> Still climbing trees in the Hesperides?...

The exercise can also be very productive when used on a scene with more than one character. First, it makes the actors share their thoughts in a remarkable way, breaking all the preconceived patterns: plus the enjoyment that is had from using their imagination to build something spills over into the language and fills it with a different energy. It can also be used aggressively for characters with opposing ideas: for as one character builds, so the other can take it down, or even use it for his or her own structure: you can turn this exercise in so many ways. However you work it, the language becomes active and tactile.

To do this on the following scene in *Troilus and Cressida* (III ii), would highlight the male/female divide just in the very choice of imagery.

TROILUS: O that I thought it could be in a woman –
            As, if it can, I will presume in you –

To feed for aye her lamp and flames of love,
To keep her constancy in plight and youth,
Outliving beauty's outward, with a mind
That doth renew swifter than blood decays!
Or that persuasion could but thus convince me,
That my integrity and truth to you
Might be affronted with the match and weight
Of such a winnowed purity in love –
How were I then uplifted! But alas,
I am as true as truth's simplicity,
And simpler than the infancy of truth.

CRESSIDA: In that I'll war with you.

TROILUS: O virtuous fight
When right with right wars who shall be most right!
True swains in love shall in the world to come
Approve their truths by Troilus; when their rhymes,
Full of protest, of oaths, and big compare,
Want similes, truth tired with iteration –
As true as steel, as plantage to the moon,
As sun to day, as turtle to her mate,
As iron to adamant, as earth to th'centre, –
Yet, after all comparisons of truth,
As truth's authentic author to be cited
'As true as Troilus' shall crown up the verse
And sanctify the numbers.

CRESSIDA: Prophet may you be!
If I be false, or swerve a hair from truth
When time is old and hath forget itself,
When waterdrops have worn the stones of Troy,
And blind oblivion swallowed cities up,
And mighty states characterless are grated
To dusty nothing, yet let memory,
From false to false, among false maids in love,
Upbraid my falsehood! When they've said 'As false
As air, as water, wind, or sandy earth,
As fox to lamb, as wolf to heifer's calf.

Pard to the hind, or step dame to her son' –
Yea, let them say, to stick the heart of falsehood,
'As false as Cressid'.

Covert Relations

If you have a situation where the characters are close, perhaps planning something which they do not want discovered – as with the Hermia/Lysander scene (pages 113–14) – and they need to express something important with speed and clarity, the following strategy is a great one to use – even if rather complicated to explain!

- Place the characters in the centre of the space – as at the centre of the stage.

- On each side at a slight distance, as at the side of the stage, should be a space where two volunteers from the group can walk up and down – from upstage to downstage and then back. Place two chairs at a little distance from each other on each of those walkways to mark the places at which the characters speaking could be heard by those walking.

- Ask two members of the group to walk up and down – one on each side, as at the edge of the stage – and ask them to do this at random while the actors play the scene.

- Now as the main characters are working the scene, they each must keep an eye on the spaces between the chairs on either side, and when one of the walkers is in one of those spaces, the actor must stop talking – for they can be overheard.

- This gives the actors that awareness of danger, and makes them very careful and precise as they speak – yet speedy, for the information has to be got over as quickly as possible: immediately the danger and the cost of what they are saying becomes apparent.

- The words become 'special' though not forced – a useful thing for us all to hear in this time of over-naturalistic throwaway speaking. The other thing is that, because of the randomness of the moments they have to stop, the literal pattern of the sense is broken and so becomes unexpected, and this heightens the suspense. It is a particularly good exercise in making us aware of the speed and specificity of thought.

This is a very useful exercise because the need for privacy is central to so many situations within a play, and this allows the actor to experience that precision and speed in a totally practical way.

Making Contact

This following strategy is one of the most telling, for it can take us very deep into the emotional life of a character particularly if that character is alone, but needing to express quite deep feelings.

- First, let the actor start their speech somewhere in the space, and as they do so get the rest of the group to walk at random round in the space.

- The actor speaking should then go up to one person in the group as they are walking and speak a phrase of the text to them.

- Their need is to make face to face contact with the other as they speak: the person in the group to whom the actor speaks must immediately turn away and walk on.

- The actor then tries again with another person but the same thing happens – and so on until the end of the speech.

- By the time they reach the end this dismissal by the group becomes very disturbing for the actor involved, and although they are totally aware that it is an exercise, it makes that sense of the character's aloneness very real – and they will hear how the words themselves have changed.

- Whatever the situation, the vulnerability of the character will emerge very clearly.

Again this could be worked on several of the speeches we have looked at so far, Isabella for instance. But I suppose the most telling one would be that of Ophelia after her encounter with *Hamlet*, in III i. We looked at this speech in the Workshop session (page 61), both for the metre and for the vowel lengths.

- This exercise highlights her predicament, for she knows that she has no one to talk to – for no one would understand.

- And this of course is confirmed by Claudius and Polonius coming in having listened to the whole scene from, and Polonius at one point saying –

> How now, Ophelia?
> You need not tell us what Lord Hamlet said,
> We heard it all.

This strategy has a particularly powerful effect, for it makes her aloneness so real.

- If working on a duologue where one character wants to make another character listen and respond, as he or she speaks you ask the character who is resistant to turn and walk away.

- If need be they can take it to extremes and walk out of the room – whatever happens, the speaker has to follow them and make them listen.

- The frustration for the actor speaking, and their need to get their thoughts across to the other person, feeds the language and makes it very strong.

A great scene that comes to mind would be Arthur pleading with Hubert at the end of IV i in *King John*: Hubert has been constrained by King John to kill his nephew the young Arthur, Duke of Brittany, fearing his political power. The scene between Arthur and Hubert is very moving.

Round the Table

For a scene between three or more characters, where serious issues are being discussed and there is a lot at stake, it can be very helpful to do this following exercise round a table.

- First, put whatever table you have in the middle of the space – it should be as large as possible: put a good number of chairs round it, at least twice as many as there are characters in the scene.

- The actors should start by sitting at the table with spaces between them but, as the scene gets going, each actor can move to another chair, either toward or away from the actor who is speaking, however their inclination takes them.

- It is very revealing how this highlights the different alignments the characters have with each other: we hear their nuances of thought, and their insecurities.

A particularly good scene to work this on is in *Julius Caesar*, I ii, after Caesar and his followers have gone out: Casca, Brutus and Cassius are left. In the scene they are feeling each other out regarding their attitudes to Caesar, each with a secret but unspoken thought – that he should be killed. The times are dangerous.

This exercise of moving towards or away from each other clarifies their alignments, and the possible dangers: it also highlights the underlying irony which is there in the wryness of the language – and in its prose rhythms.

Barriers

All drama is about opposing motives, opposing needs, between characters, and these differences erupt in scenes where the characters are trying to resolve the issues, and so are often by nature quite explosive.

Always an excellent way to explore the possibilities of a scene is to build barriers. It can be a barrier to defend yourself, or a barrier to block someone else in, or it can simply be a barrier to block out what you do not want to see: you can collude in building the barrier, or you can be obstructive – you have to choose whichever relates to the scene best. What is good is that the barrier personifies the block that is there between the characters and the situation, plus the building of the barrier, with whatever is in the space, can become rough and physically demanding – all the qualities within the character or characters at the time, thus making the thoughts difficult to express.

This would work extremely well in the scene in *Romeo and Juliet* when Capulet explodes at Juliet's refusal to marry Paris, the husband he has chosen for her (page 80). The scene is III v, and can be taken from Capulet's entrance. It is a particularly violent scene, though short, and you could take it through this way:

- As soon as Capulet hears of her refusal to marry Paris, he starts to build a barrier round to fence her in.
- Juliet immediately tries to break the barrier down, for she wants to talk over the situation and explain her feelings – she is helped by the Nurse.
- The more she tries to take the barrier down, the quicker and rougher Capulet becomes in building it up.
- Where Lady Capulet is in all this has to be discovered – but it will be quite rough.
- When Juliet and the Nurse are left alone, they may want to put everything back in its place – or they may just want to sit on the floor.

Manipulation

This is basically about persuasion, trying to make someone do something against their will and judgement: it will therefore be a dialogue between the person who is trying to persuade and get their own way, and the person they are trying to persuade and who is resistant – the manipulator and the manipulated.

For example, while the character who is being manipulated is speaking their text, the manipulator could try to get them to lie down – make a comfortable space for them on the floor with anything they can find, and try to get them to settle. This is disempowering and thus can affect the character being manipulated quite profoundly, though in different ways – either by making them acquiescent and going with the invitation, or by opposing it and becoming quite rebellious. It can bring out the violence which may be there in the text. There are many variations on this depending on the characters and the situation – but it will always open up interesting possibilities, in particular the often ambivalent motives within a character.

I worked this exercise once on *King Lear*, at the end of II iv: Goneril and Regan have been trying to persuade Lear that he has no need of any of his followers, for when he visits either of them they will each provide for all his needs. It is a long and complicated scene.

- As they reasoned with him, so they found a comfortable spot and tried to get him to lie down even as he resisted, covering him with whatever they could find.
- They also started to undress him.

Here is the end of that part of the scene – before Lear goes out:

GONERIL: Hear me, my lord:
What need you five-and-twenty, ten or five,
To follow, in a house where twice so many
Have a command to tend you?
REGAN: What need one?

Finally it became so unbearable for Lear that he sprang up, throwing everything away from him and said:

LEAR: O, reason not the need! Our basest beggars
Are in the poorest things superfluous.
Allow not nature more than nature needs –
Man's life is cheap as beasts.

Of course in the scene Lear rebels against his daughters quite violently, we hear it in the text, but this exercise gave the actor playing Lear an intensity and anger which erupted in an extraordinary way. Although a game, the sense of disempowerment went rather near the bone and the reaction was quite fierce – it certainly took him onto the heath. What was good was that the actor retained that fierceness throughout the run of the play.

Arguing and Questioning

One final exercise which is quick, but can provoke different ideas and energies:

- On a solo speech, ask the actor to work through their speech, and ask the rest of the group to stand round the actor and argue with them as they speak, or question them – depending on the situation.

- This is provocative and forces the actor to clarify what they are saying in a very positive and active way.

To Sum Up

These are the strategies I have evolved so far. For me they are very important because they connect the actor with the language and its sound in a totally real and personal way, free from any constraints of the mind. They so often throw up an unexpected nuance of meaning. It is that freedom we are after.

From the director's perspective;

i It is often quite difficult to decide which strategy to follow: there is just no logic in this, you have to go with your instinct according to the scene and the actors, and if the exercise is not working in the way you expected, change to one of the others – you will always get something out of it.

ii It is most important that the work is layered through the rehearsal period, for the further you get into rehearsal the more deeply it will inform.

For the actor:

i By physicalising the underlying motive of the text in some way, you are able to find your own personal connection to the language in a different, and perhaps more profound way.

ii Because you often discover things in an exercise that are helpful, you may worry that you will not retain those resonances of thought and feeling in performance: but that will sort itself out as you continue with the run of the play.

I suppose what is the centre for me is that all the strategies are about finding and clarifying the thoughts: thoughts, even negative ones, always lead somewhere. It is those initial thoughts which give rise to the feelings, and not the other way round, and this is so important for now when we are still heavily influenced by Method acting from across the Atlantic and their interpretation of Stanislavsky where emotion rules: and when we are also swamped by endless sentimentality on television. It is how we *think* that is interesting, and not how we *feel*.

SECTION THREE
Voice and Space

Chapter Six

WORKING THE SPACE

THIS CHAPTER IS IN two sections. The first focuses on collective work which can be done as a group in the rehearsal room in order to open out the language and our awareness of space: and later of course in the theatre or studio where you are going to perform. In the second part we will be looking at the specifics of the space itself – what to look out for, and how to get the best out of it.

Collective Speaking

As we all know putting on a play is a collective act, a co-operation between writer, director, designer, composer, voice person and actor, plus all those working around the project. I believe for the acting company it is particularly important to build on this sense of collective understanding and response. This is why I think it is so valuable to spend some time on text other than the one in hand, so that both the act of listening and the act of responding become integral to the work in rehearsal. Rehearsal time is always at a premium, I know; however, because this work tunes our ears to the subtleties of rhythm and cadence in a very focused and particular way, in the end I believe it actually quickens the rehearsal process.

The work falls into three areas:

i Telling a story while moving round in the space. This can be wonderfully releasing for the actor for, by walking or running round as you speak, the language takes on an energy and muscularity of its own: sharing the story round in this way, we are constantly alerted to new rhythms and images – plus we hear the size of the language without it being forced.

ii Passing a text round quietly in a circle, quite still. This is quite the opposite, for it is simple and quiet and makes us listen and respond: we take on each other's energy, but we keep our own voice and truth.

iii Building something together: we have already looked at this strategy of building a structure in a rehearsal situation, but it can also be very rewarding to do it as a group exercise.

Story-telling

In theatre we are always telling a story whether it be in a modern or classical idiom, and that awareness has to be inside the actor. He or she may be performing in a minimal laconic style, Beckett or Pinter, or in flowery Restoration comedy, but there must always be that awareness of something being carried forward, a feeling or a circumstance, and that is reflected in the voice, or should I say the collective voice, for each character is involved. How we listen is of the essence – it must always be active.

I have covered this area quite fully in *Text in Action*, looking in detail at several texts which can be used for this – one of them being the speeches of the Player King in *Hamlet*, for it is real primal story-telling, and it makes a great beginning to this collective work – you cannot but enjoy it.

Hamlet starts the speech off –

HAMLET: 'The rugged Pyrrhus, he whose sable arms,
Black as his purpose, did the night resemble
When he lay couchèd in th'ominous horse,
Hath now this dread and black complexion smeared
With heraldry more dismal. Head to foot
Now is he total gules, horridly tricked
With blood of fathers, mothers, daughters, sons,
Baked and impasted with the parching streets,
That lend a tyrannous and a damnèd light

To their lord's murder; roasted in wrath and fire,
And thus o'er-sizèd with coagulate gore,
With eyes like carbuncles, the hellish Pyrrhus
Old grandsire Priam seeks.'
So, proceed you.

POLONIUS: 'Fore God, my lord, well spoken, with good accent and
good discretion.[1]

Polonius always has to make a judgement!

I like to begin by getting the group to work this first speech together – finding their voice in it, as it were. So –

- Let them read it through on their own a couple of times to get the sense: then, to get the breath and resonance working, let them sit on the floor, and with their hands on their stomach below the waist, get them to use it as a breathing exercise, working it a couple of times through, connecting the voice with the breath: they should breathe at – 'horse', 'streets', 'dismal' and 'murder'. In the end they should be able to do it on three breaths – ie, at 'dismal' and 'murder'.

- And then to the end: as they do this, they can bounce on the floor feeling their own vibration in the body – particularly in the seat and chest.

- Then to find the muscularity of the speech together, get them to kneel on all fours speaking it into the floor, but concentrating on the muscularity of the text, and feeling the vibration of those voiced consonants – eg,
'rugged' – 'sable arms' –
'horridly tricked'
'dread and black complexion smeared...'
'total gules' – 'coagulate gore'

- Then get each actor to choose a phrase that they particularly enjoy, and together roll around on the floor saying their own chosen phrase, and feeling the vibration in their bodies as they speak: it is great to do this because it gives each actor a feeling

---

1 *Hamlet*, II ii.

142

of freedom with the language, plus a sense of owning it: then work through it together, finding the collective story-telling and cadence of the speech, whilst keeping the involvement of the whole voice.

Now, ignoring Polonius, go on to this next piece of the story which is very simply told, and has great variety of movement within each line.

- Read it through together first so that the story is clear to everyone, then divide it up and give each actor a line, or line and a half, as the story dictates, but something that can be remembered easily – I would suggest the following breaks, but it will depend on how many actors there are in the group.

FIRST PLAYER:
              'Anon he finds him,
Striking too short at Greeks. His antique sword, /
Rebellious to his arm, lies, where it falls,
Repugnant to command. / Unequal matched
Pyrrhus at Priam drives, in rage strikes wide, /
But with the whiff and wind of his fell sword
Th'unnerved father falls. / Then senseless Ilium,
Seeming to feel this blow, with flaming top /
Stoops to his base, and with a hideous crash
Takes prisoner Pyrrhus' ear. / For lo! His sword,
Which was declining on the milky head /
Of reverend Priam, seemed i'th'air to stick. /
So as a painted tyrant Pyrrhus stood, /
And like a neutral to his will and matter
Did nothing. /
But as we often see, against some storm, /
A silence in the heavens, the rack stand still, /
The bold winds speechless, and the orb below
As hush as death; / anon the dreadful thunder
Doth rend the region; / so after Pyrrhus' pause,
A rousèd vengeance sets him new a-work, /
And never did the Cyclops' hammers fall /
On Mars's armour, forged for proof eterne, /

> With less remorse than Pyrrhus' bleeding sword
> Now falls on Priam. /
> Out, out, thou strumpet Fortune! All you gods, /
> In general synod, take away her power! /
> Break all the spokes and fellies from her wheel, /
> And bowl the round nave down the hill of heaven,
> As low as to the fiends!'[1]

How one breaks a text like this up is always tricky, because the phrases vary so much in length and you do want to keep the sense clear, plus it depends on how many actors there are in the group – however I have indicated the possible breaks.

- The group should then walk around the space speaking their own lines – give them plenty of time to do this, for the better they know their own lines the more fruitful will be the end result.

- Then get them in a circle and ask them to speak it round in order several times: when you feel they are sure with this, let them run round the space saying their lines in order – they will have to lift them above the noise of the running. When the time is right, get them to continue running but when it gets to their own line they must jump onto something, eg, a chair or a table, as they speak: next time they run they could make a gesture which reflects their moment in the story.

- There are such wonderful moments –
  'in rage strikes wide' –
  'But with the whiff and wind of he fell sword
  Th'unnerved father falls...'
  'Takes prisoner Pyrrhus' ear'

- Do not be afraid to let them experiment with this more than once, it always takes two or three goes to really find one's connection with the words and the heightened and expansive imagery, and be excited by it. There is just such a release for the actor to find these words through their whole body.

---

1 *Hamlet*, II ii.

- The next step is to form a circle, quite a wide circle, and ask them to tell the story again: but this time to concentrate on telling the story as simply as they want. When they speak they need to come into the middle of the circle and tell their section of it round to the group

- It can be as loud or as quiet as they wish: the aim is to keep the story going plus involve everyone in their part of it.

- This way we hopefully keep the physical alertness that was found when running about, but now as a group being aware of the image and those moments in the story which affect the listener: after all, the pictures which are recounted are no more horrible or exaggerated than what we read in the newspaper each day.

- There are marvellous moments of stillness in this passage where the lines seem suspended in the air –
'seemed to stick…'
'So as a painted tyrant Pyrrhus stood,
And like a neutral to his will and matter
Did nothing.'
– these last two words taking the whole line.

We obviously notice but do not speak the interjections of Polonius and Hamlet: it is very pleasing to note how Polonius always has to make a comment as the critic, he seems only to operate from the left side of his brain so that his imagination is not engaged: this tells us a lot about his character – literal and likes to organise.

We then go on to the last part of the speech starting with:

FIRST PLAYER: 'But who, ah woe! Had seen the mobled Queen –'
HAMLET: 'The mobled Queen'?
POLONIUS: That's good. 'Mobled Queen' is good.
FIRST PLAYER: 'Run barefoot, up and down…'[1]

We now need to work through it, again leaving out Polonius' critique regarding the word 'mobled'.

---

1   *Hamlet*, II ii.

FIRST PLAYER: 'But who, ah woe, had seen the mobled Queen,
    Run barefoot up and down, threatening the flames
    With bisson rheum; a clout upon that head
    Where late the diadem stood: and for a robe,
    About her lank and all o'er-teemèd loins,
    A blanket in the alarm of fear caught up –
    Who this had seen, with tongue in venom steeped
    'Gainst Fortune's state would treason have
     pronounced.
    But if the gods themselves did see her then,
    When she saw Pyrrhus make malicious sport
    In mincing with his sword her husband's limbs,
    The instant burst of clamour that she made,
    Unless things mortal move them not at all,
    Would have made milch the burning eyes of heaven
    And passion in the gods.'[1]

This section of the story has the most wonderful cadence to it, and I believe has great value if the group speaks it through together for, without over-dramatising it or making it declamatory, we hear how delicately the cadence of the speech lifts the story through, plus we clock those images which are momentarily out of real time –

       a clout upon that head
   Where late the diadem stood:

I think it starts quite low, fulfilling those long vowels –

   But who, ah woe! Had seen the mobled Queen...

the thoughts then lift through quite quickly and come to a climax on –

   would treason have pronounced.

It then starts again quite low and unhurried –

   But if the gods themselves did see her then...

---

1 *Hamlet*, II ii.

and lifts on each line through to –

> The instant burst of clamour that she made…

and there it suspends a moment, hangs in the air, to allow us to think of that other power above with –

> Unless things mortal move them not at all…

and the story comes to fruition on the last line and a half –

> Would have made milch the burning eyes of heaven
> And passion in the gods.

Now everyone hears things differently, and I have laid out how I hear it. But the point is there is a music there in the story, a cadence that moves us when we speak, which is to do with how one thought, one part of the story, lifts to the next, and so quickens the interest of the listener: we also have to give full value to the texture of the vowels and consonants – we need to take this on board and be bold with it: we have to hear how the cadence and texture of the language fulfils the meaning – and vice versa.

Polonius' next comment –

> Look whe'er he has not turned colour, and has tears
> in's eyes…

is so often played to be funny, but I think it has a profound implication, and that is that the very act of speaking words can be moving for the speaker, whether on stage or in real life.

As I have already said this group work is laid out fully in *Text in Action* which contains two other examples: verses from *Rape of Lucrece*, which is a great story to tell and which I have gone into very fully. Also one section of Lorca's *Lament for Ignacio Sanchez Mejias*, and this I will look at again in a later section of this chapter (page 156), when we look at work in the theatre space itself. Of course there are many poems you can use in this way, such as a section of Coleridge's *The Rime of the Ancient Mariner*, or of Tennyson's *The Lady of Shalott*, and there are many ballads which are great to do.

Passing Round Text

I have always found that a really effective and simple way to start the work on text is to speak a poem, line by line, round in a circle. The choice of poem is up to one's individual preference, but the important thing is to work a good mixture of styles. It should not be too long, so that as you speak it round in the circle several times people in the group will get familiar with it, and also will get different lines each time round. As you do this each person starts to give themselves up to its sound as well as its meaning, and so much emerges unexpectedly. We need a good mixture, and it is great to start with one of Donne's simpler love lyrics such as his 'Song' which begins

> Sweetest love I do not go
> For weariness of thee...[1]

or the following poem of Herrick:

To Anthea, Who May Command Him Anything

> Bid me to live, and I will live
>   Thy Protestant to be:
> Or bid me love, and I will give
>   A loving heart to thee.
>
> A heart as soft, a heart as kind,
>   A heart as sound and free,
> As in the whole world thou canst find
>   That heart I'll give to thee.
>
> Bid that heart stay, and it will stay
>   To honour thy decree:
> Or bid it languish quite away,
>   And 't shall do so for thee.

---

1   The full text can be found in such editions as John Donne, *The Complete English Poems*, ed A J Smith (Penguin Books: Harmondsworth, 1996), 78–9; and *Selected Poetry*, ed John Carey (Oxford University Press: Oxford, 1996), 90–1.

Bid me to weep, and I will weep
　While I have eyes to see:
And, having none, yet will I keep
　A heart to weep for thee.

Bid me despair, and I'll despair
　Under that cypress-tree:
Or bid me die, and I will dare
　E'en death to die for thee.

Thou art my life, my love, my heart,
　The very eyes of me:
And hast command of every part
　To live and die for thee.[1]

I realise you may possibly think this is irrelevant, and about a little fancy verse speaking – so what is it about? It is simply this: it allows the actor time to listen to rhythms and spaces, and how these are tuned to the thoughts which are then lifted through in a very subtle way. I think it is always good to do something of a classical mode, because the unfamiliar language sharpens our ears, and often gives us unexpected pleasure. Perhaps it reminds us where we came from.

But of course modern text is central to our work, and the choice of poems is endless. Modern work is particularly good because it does not necessarily follow a verse pattern, it is rather through the length and spacing of the lines that we hear and understand something beyond the literal meaning. This poem of Lawrence Ferlinghetti illustrates this perfectly:

In Goya's greatest scenes we seem to see
　　　　　　　　　　　the people of the world
　　　exactly at the moment when
　　　　　they first attained the title of
　　　　　　　　　　　'suffering humanity'
　　　They writhe upon the page

1　Robert Herrick, *Hesperides*, XCVI.

FROM WORD TO PLAY

in a veritable rage
of adversity
Heaped up
groaning with babies and bayonets
under cement skies
in an abstract landscape of blasted trees
bent statues bats' wings and beaks
slippery gibbets
cadavers and carnivorous cocks
and all the final hollering monsters
of the
'imagination of disaster'
they are so bloody real
it is as if they really still existed

And they do

Only the landscape is changed

They still are ranged along the roads
plagued by legionaires
false windmills and demented roosters

They are the same people
only further from home
on freeways fifty lanes wide
on a concrete continent
spaced with bland billboard
illustrating imbecile illusions of happiness

The scene shows fewer tumbrils
but more maimed citizens
in painted cars
and they have strange license plates

150

and engines
　　　　that devour America[1]

It is an angry poem, and this anger surfaces both in the imagery and in the way the lines erupt: it is a perfect example of how our sensitivity to timing and phrasing can impact on the meaning and give it power.

As I have said, the choice of poems is endless, and we all have our favourites: but most certainly those of T S Eliot and W H Auden yield so much in terms of spareness and their underlying ambience – and I have found it very difficult to choose. There are also some great translations from the poetry of Neruda, Cavafy, Günter Grass, Enzensberger *et al.* But perhaps, even for modern text, we should look at something more formal, so here is a poem of W B Yeats:

John Kinsella's Lament for Mrs Mary Moore

A bloody and a sudden end,
　Gunshot or a noose,
For Death who takes what man would keep,
　Leaves what man would lose.
He might have had my sister,
　My cousins by the score,
But nothing satisfied the fool
　But my dear Mary Moore,
None other knows what pleasures man
　At table or in bed.
What shall I do for pretty girls
Now my old bawd is dead?

Though stiff to strike a bargain,
　Like an old Jew man,
Her bargain struck we laughed and talked
　And emptied many a can;
And O! but she had stories,

1　Lawrence Ferlinghetti, *A Coney Island of the Mind*, (New York: New Directions, 1955), 9–10.

Though not for the priest's ear,
To keep the soul of man alive,
  Banish age and care,
And being old she put a skin
  On everything she said.
What shall I do for pretty girls
Now my old bawd is dead?

The priests have got a book that says
  But for Adam's sin
Eden's Garden would be there
  And I there within.
No expectation fails there,
  No pleasing habit ends,
No man grows old, no girl grows cold,
  But friends walk by friends.
Who quarrels over halfpennies
  That plucks the trees for bread?
What shall I do for pretty girls
Now my old bawd is dead?[1]

Here is anger and love intermixed: and we hear it in the rhythm which is very powerful, and which reminds us what effect that incantational beat can have on us as we speak it, and therefore how it can affect the listener.

Building Structures

We have already looked at this in the last chapter, but I want to bring it up again because it is an excellent way of getting a group to discover things in the language together.

- Each person would take a line, and when their turn came to speak, they would have to add something to the structure – anything that they could find: if it were Gaunt's speech in *Richard II* (II i), it would have to be a structure to England: or

---

1 W B Yeats, *The Collected Poems,* (London: Wordsworth Poetry Library, 2000) 289–90.

if Queen Margaret in *Richard III* (I iii), it would be a structure to anger and scorn. If you worked it on the speech of Berowne from *Love's Labour's Lost* that we have already looked at (page 128), it would have to be a structure to love.

- You could also work it on a poem.

- The benefit is this: because you are handling something with your hands the words take on another quality – they become tactile and in a way three dimensional.

None of these exercises need take long, and the more frequently you can include them in rehearsal the more quickly the actors will respond. I firmly believe work of this kind enriches the acting process, and puts the text at the centre of the play.

The Space Itself

Now we need to consider the space we will be working in, and this is never simple for, whether large or small, proscenium, thrust or traverse, each space has its own acoustic quality. The crucial thing is that actors are given time to experiment vocally in that space so that they find their own voice and feel comfortable with it.

Once the technical rehearsal is over, time must be given for finding the acoustic of the space, and what is necessary for it, so that what has been found in rehearsal is not lost.

What is necessary is seldom to do with increase of volume. To think of audibility in terms of volume is always misleading; it is nearly always to do with:

i The muscularity of the consonants, and one's intention to reach the edges of the space and lift the language through.

ii It is also about pitch: if a space is large and rather resonant, a low-pitched voice will get lost. You have to give the actors time to hear this and to adjust accordingly.

iii Awareness of where the audience is placed: if, as in the Swan Theatre in Stratford, the balconies are high and vertical, the actor has to be conscious of this, not by looking directly at them, but rather by keeping the head lifted to an extent so that they feel at all times included.

If working on a proscenium arch stage, one's focus is quite clear – to reach out to the auditorium. However, the shape of the set and the materials used in it, can make a considerable difference. If the set is mainly made of wood and brick, the resultant sound can be over-bright, so that the actor needs to adjust the volume and pitch to suit it. If the set consists mainly of plastic and absorbent material, then the need is to lift the pitch slightly and sharpen the consonants.

If working on a thrust stage, or in a studio theatre, or in a traverse space, the actor will nearly always have their back to one section of their audience. There is nothing specific you can do about this, but again it is always about being aware of where the audience is sitting and making sure that the physicality of the language is reaching everywhere.

To test out the space there is nothing better than to take a piece of text, and work through it as in the exercises at the beginning of this chapter. If you are in a large space, and you have time, the Player King speech is particularly good: they can run round the space with it, jumping on seats, etc, and so get a sense of belonging there, and that everyone can be included. They then can end up at the edges of the theatre, speaking it as quietly as possibly, but making sure they are heard: it is important to find out how quiet you can be, but of course always remembering that an audience will take up some of that sound.

Here are two pieces of text which are rewarding to do. The first is from Blake's *Auguries of Innocence*:

> To see a World in a Grain of Sand
> And a Heaven in a Wild Flower,
> Hold Infinity in the palm of your hand

6: WORKING THE SPACE

And Eternity in an hour.

A Robin Red breast in a Cage
Puts all Heaven in a Rage.
A dove house fill'd with Doves & Pigeons
Shudders Hell thro' all its regions.
A Dog starv'd at his Master's Gate
Predicts the ruin of the State.
A Horse misus'd upon the Road
Calls to Heaven for Human blood.
Each outcry of the hunted Hare
A fibre from the Brain does tear.
A Skylark wounded in the wing,
A Cherubim does cease to sing.
The Game Cock clip'd & arm'd for fight
Does the Rising Sun affright.
Every Wolf's and Lion's howl
Raises from Hell a Human Soul.
The wild deer wand'ring here & there
Keeps the Human Soul from Care.
The Lamb misus'd breeds Public strife,
And yet forgives the Butcher's Knife.
The Bat that flits at close of Eve
Has left the Brain that won't Believe.
The Owl that calls upon the Night
Speaks the Unbeliever's fright.
He who shall hurt the little Wren
Shall never be belov'd by Men.
He who the Ox to wrath hath mov'd
Shall never be by Woman lov'd.
The wanton Boy that kills the Fly
Shall feel the Spider's enmity.
He who torments the Chafer's sprite
Weaves a bower in endless Night.
The Catterpiller on the Leaf
Repeats to thee thy Mother's grief.

Kill not the Moth nor Butterfly,
For the Last Judgement draweth nigh.
He who shall train the Horse to War
Shall never pass the Polar Bar.
The Beggar's Dog & Widow's Cat,
Feed them & thou wilt grow fat.
The Gnat that sings at his Summer's song
Poison gets from Slander's tongue.
The poison of the Snake & Newt
Is the sweat of Envy's Foot.
The Poison of the Honey Bee
Is the Artist's Jealousy.
The Prince's Robes & Beggar's Rags
Are Toadstools on the Miser's Bags.
A truth that's told with bad intent
Beats all the Lies you can invent.
It is right it should be so;
Man was made for Joy & Woe,
And when this we rightly know,
Thro' the World we safely go.
Joy & Woe are woven fine
A Clothing for the Soul divine.[1]

This is just about half of the whole poem, but you can use any part of it: it is a great piece to on work with the group in the space, each person taking two lines. It is both thought-provoking and simple, and of course very Blakean, and therefore each person can contribute their own truth through it: it can be like a discussion. It also puts you in touch with a rare spirit.

This next, already mentioned, is by Federico Garcia Lorca: the second part of his *Lament for Ignacio Sanchez Mejias*, translated by A L Lloyd – it is a great translation.

---

1 *Auguries of Innocence*. The punctuation follows the Everyman edition: William Blake, *Selected Poems* (London: J M Dent & Sons, 1982), 132–3.

The Spilling of the Blood

I do not want to see it!

Tell the moon to come
for I don't want to see the blood
of Ignacio on the sand.

I do not want to see it!
The wide-open moon,
horse of the quiet clouds,
and the grey bullring of dream,
with willows at the barriers.
I do not want to see it!
For my memory scorches.
Call for the jasmines
with their little whiteness!
I do not want to see it!

The cow of the old world
passed her sad tongue
over a muzzle of blood
spilt on the sand,
and the bulls of Guisando,
half death, and half stone,
bellowed like two centuries
weary of treading the earth.
No.
I don't want to see it!

Ignacio climbs up the terraces
with all his death on his shoulders.
He looked for daybreak,
but there was no daybreak.
He seeks his own sure profile,
and a dream misleads him.
He sought his handsome body
and was faced with his unsealed blood.

Don't tell me to see it!
I don't want to feel the jet
each time with less force;
that jet that illumines
the rows of seats, and pours
over the corduroy and leather
of the thirsty multitude.
Who shouts to me to look?
Don't tell me to see it!

His eyes did not close
when he saw the horns near,
but the terrible mothers
lifted their heads.
And across the ranches
went a breath of secret voices
calling the heavenly bulls,
herd-leaders of the pallid mist.

There was no Prince in Seville
who could compare to him,
nor any sword like his sword
nor any heart so earnest.
Like a river of lions
his marvellous strength,
like a marble torso
his fine-drawn caution.
The air of Andalusian Rome
gilded his head
where his smile was a nard
of wit and of skill.
What a great bullfighter in the ring!
What a splendid mountaineer in the mountains!
How soft with the wheat-ears!
How hard with the spurs!
How tender with the dew!
How dazzling in the feria!

How tremendous with the last
banderillas of darkness!

But now he sleeps endlessly.
Now mosses and grass
are opening with sure fingers
the flower of his skull.
And his blood goes singing now,
singing by marshes and meadows,
sliding on frozen horns,
wavering soulless through the mist
stumbling on its thousand hoofs
like a long, dark sad tongue
till it forms a pool of agony
by the starry Guadalquivir.
Oh white wall of Spain!
Oh stubborn blood of Ignacio!
Oh nightingale of his veins.
No.
I don't want to see it!
There is no chalice that could hold it,
no swallows that could drink it,
no frost of light to cool it,
nor any song nor flood of lilies,
there is no glass to cover it with silver
No.
I don't want to see it.[1]

- It will depend on how many there are in the group how you divide it up.

- It works very well if you start off with everyone speaking the first four or five sections together, to find a collective voice.

- Then when it gets to the stanza beginning 'There was no prince in Seville...' it divides very well into two lines per speaker.

---

1 Federico Garcia Lorca, *Lament for Ignacio Mejias*: Part Two, 'The Spilling of the Blood', Translated by A L Lloyd.

- And from here you can take it running round in the space, jumping on seats as you speak your line, and/or making a shape or gesture with your body to convey the terrible and violent heart of the story.

- If it works out with the distribution of the lines, it is good to do the last lines together, from – 'Oh white wall of Spain…' to find that sound and that feeling as a group.

What is particularly good about this piece is that you can end up by speaking it very quietly to each other round in the space, and just simply telling the story: it proves to be very moving.

Chapter Seven

VOCAL PREPARATION

AS WITH CHAPTER SIX, I am writing this in two sections. First – I want to set out the work I think should ideally be done at the start of each rehearsal day. Second – I will lay out a fuller Voice session which can be taken through when it is appropriate, hopefully at least once a week, and which will prepare the company for performance. If you have a Voice person attached to the rehearsal, then they will not necessarily need the following, for they will lead the sessions in their own way.

Work in rehearsal

This is quite low-key work, intended specifically to prepare for rehearsal. It is not in any way about opening the sound out, or thinking about good tone and projection; rather, it is about letting the actor feel settled in their own voice, and finding its centre, and feeling comfortable with that. Once the actor feels this sense of belonging in their voice – I like to call it 'sitting down in it' – they feel a confidence in themselves, and this in turn helps to release their own creative instincts. This may sound a little fanciful, but it is in fact very true and it is worth the time given, even if you can spare only twenty minutes. So –

- With everyone standing round in the space, first, get them to have a good stretch.
- Then in their own time let them find a space on the floor and lie down – with as much room round them as possible.

- Let them then take a moment to feel their backs spread across the floor.
- When they feel comfortable with this, they should crook their legs up with their feet a little apart – this stops the waist arching up.
- They should then take a moment to feel their backs in touch with the floor all the way down: now let them feel their necks free by gently turning their heads first to one side, and then to the other quite slowly a couple of times – then back to the middle.
- Now let them roll each shoulder round once quite slowly, and then lay both shoulders out across the floor feeling them spread as wide as possible.
- Let them now take a moment to be conscious of their backs feeling long and wide.
- They should now gently shake their wrists, feeling their arms free, and put the backs of their hands on their ribs where they are at their widest.
- When all this is comfortable, get them to breathe in through the nose quite slowly, and then open their mouths and sigh out.
- They should do this several times, taking time with it, so that they feel the ribs widening along the floor, and taking care that they do not tense the shoulders or upper chest.
- When they are comfortable with this, they should breathe in, again through the nose, then breathe out through an open mouth to the count of ten, taking care that the throat is open so that they are not controlling it in the throat but rather through the muscles in the ribs:.
- Let them do this several times they now need to keep that sense of the chest being open and free.

Then instruct as follows:

- Put one hand on the stomach muscles below the waist, and take a breath down as low as you can, and then open your mouths and breathe out.
- Again breathe down into the centre, then breathe out slowly through FFF – feeling that channel of breath carrying the sound out.
- Breathe down again – then breathe out through VVV – feeling the vibration on the lips.
- Repeat this – and breathe out on ZZZ – so you feel the vibration on the tongue.
- Repeat this breathing out on a voiced SH – as in 'measure':
- When you do this, take care you do not breathe out on a note, but rather on the actual consonant vibration, so that you will feel vibration not only through your mouth and cheeks, but also in your head.

Now we should focus on the vibration in the body. So instruct as follows:

- Breathe down and then hum out for ten counts.
- Repeat this, singing quite quietly out on OO for ten – and then on OH, AH, AY and I.
- As you do this, at intervals roll your legs to one side and then to the other and then back to the middle, patting your chest to feel the vibration there, and being conscious of vibration all the way down your back into your seat.
- You can even roll round while you are doing this to feel the vibration in the whole body.
- Then, quite still, repeat the exercise singing out on those vowels – and then on any vowel you choose.
- When this is done, roll over onto your side and gently stand up.

We need now to connect with the work just done on the floor. So instruct as follows:

- Take a moment to feel the length in your back, then put one hand on your stomach below the waist, and breathe down, and then open and sigh out.
- Repeat this, breathing out on FFF, then on VVV and then on ZZZ, feeling the breath lifting the sound through.

With everyone in a circle, place an object in the middle.

- Keeping the focus on the breath from the centre, they should now breathe down and then speak the vowel OO three times on the one breath, aiming it at the object in the centre – feeling the breath starting the sound on each vowel so that there is no glottal start to the sounds.
- They should continue this on OH, AW, OW, AY, I, EE. The purpose is always to firm up that sense of the voice being carried on the breath from one's centre.
- They should repeat this – but now singing the vowels out.

The group should now sit down, and take a moment to feel their own weight on the floor. Instruct as follows:

- Get comfortable, and put your hand on your stomach below the waist.
- Breathe down, and as you breathe slightly lean back so you feel your weight going back – then as you breathe out let the weight come forward again.
- Repeat this and, sing out on OO on the outgoing breath: the singing should not be loud, for it is simply about finding how to connect with the breath, and forming that habit.
- Repeat on any of the vowels listed.
- As you do this you can bounce your seat on the floor to feel its vibration.
- And finally, still with your hand on the muscles at the centre, breathe down, then speak a few lines from a poem that you know, or from the play you are rehearsing, feeling the voice sitting down in that centre.

Each person can do this separately, but they each need to hear themselves and be conscious of their own sound: this will affirm that sense of the words coming from the centre.

Full Voice Session

Having been trained at the Central School of Speech and Drama in the mid-forties, under that great teacher Gwynneth Thurburn, I was reared on the creed that good breathing was the foundation of all voice work. Now here, in the 21st century, I still believe that 'breath is voice' – and vice-versa.

However, that does not mean to say that how we use that breath has not changed for, as I have said earlier, fashions of language are forever changing, and we certainly do not want that rather over-resonant poetic sound fashionable fifty years ago. But even so, the modern ear is still hungry for a voice that vibrates somewhere in their ears, however quietly, and draws them to listen. Although now I think we seldom use that rib breath on stage, rather we work from the muscles at the centre, yet we need to have the whole of the chest space open and free so that that resonance is the body of the voice. That is why I always start with working the ribs.

I will lay out the work as I find it, but of course it can be altered and structured to fit the particular work in hand, and your particular preferences.

- First, always, get them to have a good stretch.
- Then in their own time, let them find their own space and lie on the floor, with as much room round them as possible.
- Let them take a moment to feel their backs in touch with the floor all the way down: when their backs are comfortable they should then crook their legs up, with their feet a little apart.
- When they feel really spread, let them take one shoulder at a time and lift it off the floor – up and round and back and down.
- The same with the other shoulder.
- They should repeat this once, then lay the shoulders out and take time to feel them spread across the floor.

165

Then instruct as follows:

- Feeling the neck free, turn the head to one side, and then to the other side, then back to the middle
- Do this a couple of times.
- Now press the head very gently back into the floor, then free it and feel the difference: repeat this once.
- Now check the back is in touch with the floor all the way down: take time to become aware of the length and spread of your back, so you feel it both long and wide.
- Very gently, shake your wrists and your elbows and lay them out on the floor.
- Then, with your wrists free and your elbows wide, put the backs of your hands on your ribs at the side, where your ribs are at their widest.
- Feeling the ribs widening along the floor, breathe in gently through the nose (as this stimulates the ribs) then open your mouth wide and sigh out.
- This sigh should not make any noise for your throat should be open and free.
- Repeat this a couple of times.

Now on to sound. Instruct as follows:

- Breathe in quite easily, and hum out to a count of 10 – feeling the vibration of the hum on the lips: the jaw should feel loose for this so that the back of the throat does not get tight.
- Repeat this as you sing out on the following vowels – OO, OH, AW, AH, AY, I, EE.
- As you do this, pat your chest at times to be aware of the resonance there; also try to feel the resonance in your back and seat.
- All the time be aware that the neck and shoulders are free, and that the upper chest does not tense or lift: you can now increase the outgoing count to 15 – or even to 20.

- By doing this you are really opening the chest, for by the end of 20 counts the need for breath stimulates the ribs so that they are moving at their maximum.
- By singing out on that breath you are also gaining an awareness of the resonance that is possible, and that can be relied on.
- Now we need to check the relaxation at the back of the throat, so let the mouth drop open and, feeling the movement of the tongue and the uvula, speak – KE KE KE – several times – always being aware of the firmness of the sound and how it explodes with the pressure.
- Then open on to AH – feeling the space at the back of the throat: this is very important, for we so often tighten up in the throat, which in turn tightens up the sound, and so we need to be able to free it at will.
- Repeat this on the voiced consonant – GE GE GE – and while you do this put one hand on your chest so that you feel the vibration of the voiced GE sound on the chest as you speak.

We now need to focus on taking the breath into the centre, this is the breath we need to work with. So instruct as follows:

- Place one hand on your stomach below the waist, and breathe down as deeply as possible, and then sigh out.
- Repeat this, very gently singing out on OO – feeling the breath behind the sound.
- Repeat this on different vowel sounds, always checking the back and the spread and relaxation of the shoulders and neck.
- Repeat this by humming out for ten counts.
- While you are doing this keep your back open and free – and put one hand on your chest to feel its vibration.
- Now repeat this on – OH, then AH, then AY, then I – and then on any vowel you like.
- Each time be aware of the breath starting the sound and carrying it through.

167

- Having done this, and having become aware of centring the voice, gently roll over onto your side and stand up.

- Take a moment while standing to feel your back long and wide.

- Imagine for a moment you have a string coming down from the ceiling attached to the middle of your head – not to the back or the front but to the middle.

- Let it pull you up onto your toes, then let you down.

- Repeat this several times, so that you become aware of the length in your back.

- Now check your shoulders: lift them up and down quite briskly twice – in the end this is not helpful because it is too brisk and does not make for full relaxation.

- What is helpful is this: lift them about an inch, then gently drop them, then take a moment to let them go that extra bit.

- Repeat this a couple of times, each time taking a moment to be aware of that feeling of letting go – that is the feeling you need to remember.

- Take a moment to move your head round very gently so that there is no tension in the neck.

- Do this a couple of times – one way round and then the other.

Now while standing, we need to check on all the exercises that have been done on the floor. So instruct as follows:

- With the backs of your hands on your ribs at the side, making sure you feel them at the place where the ribs are at their widest. Breathe in fairly slowly through the nose, and then out through an open mouth for the count of ten, feeling the rib muscles controlling the outgoing breath.

- Repeat this, singing out on the vowels already listed.

- Next, put your hand on the stomach muscles below the waist.

- Now to place that feeling of the breath at the centre – breathe down and then sigh out.

- Now breathe down and out on FFF, feeling the channel of breath coming through.

- Repeat likewise on VVV, ZZZZ and the voiced SH.

- Then on one breath speak OO three times.

- Repeat on a sequence of vowels.

- As you find this breath from the centre keep checking that your shoulders and neck are free.

- Now in a circle, and with an object in the middle, breathe down, and, on the outgoing breath, speak a vowel three times aiming it at the object.

- Repeat this several times, but this time singing the vowel sounds – it might be good to give them a note – different for each vowel – always remembering that you are doing it on the one breath.

As a variation on this, and to link the work into performance mode, this exercise can be repeated:

- But now, when they have finished singing the vowels, they should run somewhere, then stop, take a breath down into the centre, focus on the object, and sing the next set of vowels.

This is a great exercise, for they are moving, then being still and finding their centre, then releasing the sound.

- It can be varied in many ways – you can get them to crouch when they sing the vowels, or to get in a very tense position, but always making sure that the sound is coming from the centre.

- This both releases and focuses the sound.

One last suggestion – a little difficult to explain, but it is simply this:

- They should divide into two equal groups, then stand in two lines facing each other, as wide apart as possible. I will call them line A and line B.

- The person at the beginning of line A chooses a vowel, and as they sing it they throw it as if it were a ball, to the person opposite in line B: that person then catches that note and that vowel as if with their hands.

- They then choose their own vowel and throw it to the next person in line A – and so on down the lines.

- It is a great exercise to do because it forces us to listen with accuracy, not just to the note, but to the quality of the sound – and respond accordingly.

- As a variation you can ask each person to invest their vowel with a message which they want to convey, or a feeling, and as they throw the vowel they throw the message: the catcher then has to respond in some way to that message – but always only on a single note.

I think we need always to foster this sense of listening as a group, for it will always contribute to the power and reality of the play.

This makes for quite a long session, but of course it does not necessarily all have to be done at one time; choices can be made according to the needs of the group and of the rehearsal. But it does set out the areas of work which I think are important and relevant to the work in hand.

APPENDIX
King Lear In Retrospect

I WOULD LIKE to end by taking a moment to reflect on my own production of *King Lear* in the old Other Place. I say old, because it had been a tin shed which housed theatre costumes and which was converted into a studio theatre by Buzz Goodbody in 1974. With both her vision and her strong political beliefs, Buzz created a space for both modern and classical work, which would change the actor/audience relationship, and create an environment in which the audience could feel a part of the work itself – it was affectionately known as the 'Tin Hut'. In 1989 it was deemed unsafe and so was pulled down. The new TOP ('The Other Place') building was unveiled in 1991, but in spite of its facilities and its elegance, it does not have qute the ambience of that original 'other' place.

In 1988 Tony Hill, who was running our Education Department at the time, asked me whether I would like to work on a Shakespeare play which would be put on at The Other Place, and around which we could arrange a number of open workshops. These workshops would focus on Shakespeare's language and would be practical, with those attending participating in the work. I agreed – a little nervously.

Looking back I realise that my choice of *King Lear* was an ambitious one, to say the least; but my reason at the time for choosing it was that the language offered such wonderful possibilities not only for the actors to work on and discover, but also to share with those coming to the workshops. I wanted to approach the play by speaking it first, and listening to the movement and texture of the language, before coming to conclusions about character, place and relationships. I wanted them to hear where the language takes us.

Because this was primarily an education project I needed, of course, to use actors who were working in the Company at the time, and this had to be on a voluntary basis. I was therefore very lucky in that the actors who volunteered for the work suited it perfectly.

Richard Haddon Haines, a tremendous South African actor, seemed to me absolutely right for the part of Lear.

Having decided on the play, my next thought was to ring Edward Bond to find out his vision of the play. I believe that every play has a centre image, an idea, a feeling, around which the play revolves, and of course Edward came up with his unique vision: he said something like this – 'It is a play where people are getting on and off trains with a lot of luggage'. And that became my centre image.

At the same time as I was getting the cast together, I approached the designer Chris Dyer, who had worked with the Company a good deal – including designing Buzz Goodbody's *Hamlet* at TOP – to see if he would be both free and willing to take on the job. Luckily for me he agreed. I knew he would be interested in working as simply as possible, and the result was brilliant – or perhaps I should say earth-shaking, as we shall see.

Our rehearsal time was unbelievably short: the press night of *The Tempest* which most of my cast were in, was delayed two weeks, and this badly cut into our rehearsal period, for very little work could be done during *The Tempest* understudy period as two of my main characters, Lear and the Fool, were understudying Prospero and Ariel, so it was hard for them; plus it limited the time at our disposal. But these difficulties were seen by the group as a challenge, and they responded to it with great enthusiasm.

I think *King Lear* is probably the greatest play ever written, I am sure I am not alone in this. But to me it is also a great Marxist play, for I do not believe it is a play about Lear getting old and losing his wits – that makes it sentimental. I believe Lear goes on a journey from first being ruler of a kingdom, then being rejected by his daughters, through madness on the heath, to finally realising that he is but a man – like any other, and that he has not fulfilled his duty as a man.

Here are four key speeches which illustrate this: first, his opening speech as the King in I i –

> Meantime we shall express our darker purpose.
> Give me the map there. Know that we have divided

> In three our kingdom; and 'tis our fast intent
> To shake all cares and business from our age,
> Conferring them on younger strengths, while we
> Unburdened crawl towards death.

Next, in II iv, after Goneril and Regan have both disempowered him by denying him his followers, he knows he must take action in order to find himself again:

>   I will do such things –
> What they are yet I know not; but they shall be
> The terrors of the earth. You think I'll weep.
> No, I'll not weep.
> I have full cause of weeping; (*Storm and tempest.*) But
>   this heart
> Shall break into a hundred thousand flaws
> Or ere I'll weep. O Fool, I shall go mad!

Thirdly, on the heath with Kent and the Fool in III iv, as he experiences the full force of the storm, he sends the Fool into the hovel –

> In, boy, go first. – You houseless poverty –
> Nay, get thee in. I'll pray and then I'll sleep.

Exit the FOOL.

> Poor naked wretches, wheresoe'er you are
> That bide the pelting of this pitiless storm,
> How shall your houseless heads and unfed sides
> Your looped and windowed raggedness, defend you
> From seasons such as these? O, I have ta'en
> Too little care of this! Take physic, pomp;
> Expose thyself to feel what wretches feel,
> That thou mayst shake the superflux to them
> And show the heavens more just.

Here, the realisation of what poverty really means, and his own failure in attending to it, becomes apparent to him.

Lastly, a little later in the scene, after Edgar has entered disguised as Poor Tom, Lear says to him –

> Is man no more than this? Consider him well. Thou owest the worm no silk, the beast no hide, the sheep no wool, the cat no perfume. Ha! Here's three on's are sophisticated. Thou art the thing itself! Unaccommodated man is no more but such a poor, bare, forked animal as thou art. Off, off, you lendings! Come, unbutton here. (*He tears off his clothes.*)

And so he embraces his own nakedness, his own situation of having nothing.

There are two other lines which always remain with me: Lear's

> Is there any cause in nature that makes these hard hearts?[1]

and Edgar's

> The worst is not,
> So long as we can say 'This is the worst'.[2]

But the centre line of the play for me has to be Gloucester's words:

> So distribution should undo excess,
> And each man have enough.[3]

So how to make this huge play work in a small studio space, with limited resources and a very limited rehearsal time: that was my journey. We had to create the world through the language. I am just going to set out two instances of the work we did.

The first was this: at the end of the second week after we had worked on each scene, and although the actors did not know their lines completely, I asked them to run the play through to clarify their own story line, and to work out their particular character's journeys. But I asked them to do it in a very special way: with the help of our resourceful Stage Management, each actor had a lot of

---

1 *King Lear*, III vi.
2 *King Lear*, IV i.
3 *King Lear*, IV i.

luggage, cases and boxes, etc, and I asked them to work through the play in the order of their own scenes. If scenes in the play were played simultaneously in time, then they were played simultaneously in the space, but at no time could they leave the building – they had to keep on the move carrying their luggage round the space. As you will obviously gather, this strategy was inspired by Edward Bond's words. At the same time I gave each actor a simple task to do at some time during the run: for instance, I asked the Fool to tell at least two jokes out to the audience while running the play.

The result was chaotic, but in a very positive way, for with it came a great sense of the urgency of the play. King Lear was thrown off centre stage, and scenes kept erupting all over the place. At one point Cordelia, played in Stratford by Maureen Beattie, drove off in her Fiat with the King of France, and when she returned she sent letters to Kent via the Stage Manager. This may seem absurd, but it most definitely made her aware of her distance from Lear and her need to make contact with him. I also wanted us all to get a sense of the land and the spaces they had to travel between castles, and also of the nameless inhabitants of that land. The actors became totally immersed in their own story through the play, and we were made aware of the extraordinary dynamic of that journey and of the distance travelled. That awareness stayed with them throughout rehearsal.

Perhaps the key work was done on the storm, which evolved through the whole rehearsal period: it started like this, as Lear began his speech to the storm –

Blow, winds, and crack your cheeks! Rage! Blow!...[1]

the actors would surround him and throw the words back at him. But as we got further into rehearsal it got rougher for, as well as bombarding him with words, perhaps sentences from their own characters, they would also throw light objects at him to represent twigs and leaves, etc, so that the storm was palpable to Lear, both

---

1 *King Lear*, III ii.

by the noise around him, and the words in his own head. It became a storm both inside and outside himself.

Tim Oliver, who was our Sound Designer, recorded all this: sometimes the words were whispered, sometimes shouted, and he remembers that at one point when he was recording, an actor sneezed, and this became the noise which accompanied the blinding of Gloucester. The recorded sounds were distorted, either by slowing them down or speeding them up. Tim was extremely imaginative in the way he worked all this, and in the subliminal way it was used throughout the play: he was also able to give a 'sound' presence to the hundred knights.

Now for the design. Chris Dyer wrote at the time:

> The design 'idea' came after the main staging had been decided on. What should the map be? Why not draw it on the floor? Seems a good idea and a rough drawing was done. It then becomes obvious that what should happen is for the pieces of the map to break and fall apart, creating different layers and planes.

And that is exactly what happened, the cement stage floor broke into three pieces, and it was quite literally an earth-shifting moment, for it took us right into the world of the heath: it also spoke vividly of the divided nation and the broken world of Lear's mind. No image could have expressed this more potently.

Now to say something about Richard Haddon Haines: he entered into the work in a most remarkable way. At the beginning he gave out a character with a great zest for life, who bonded strongly with his knights: it was indeed a very masculine world, something which I think is interesting in terms of his relationship with his daughters. His relationship with the Fool, played by Patrick Miller, was particularly real and tender. Throughout the play we felt his inner strength: he was never made to feel comfortable, and was always fighting something off in the storm, but he responded always in a very positive way. It was particularly good because we were never conscious of him playing an old man, rather someone who loved life, albeit not in the prime of his life: and when it came to the storm, even in his madness, he fought it. With his final reunion with Cordelia, it was never sentimental, but rather a very positive moment.

I learnt so much from this experience: the actors were all totally responsive to the work, which was after all very different from the usual rehearsal process, and because it was initially an education project, the pressure was taken off them regarding being ready for performance – though when the time did come we were indeed ready. Also because nothing specific regarding design or sound had been decided on before the Company got together, it was an exceptionally creative experience collectively.

I also had strong support from Katie Mitchell, who was then one of the Assistant Directors in the Company, and who volunteered to work on the project. Katie threw in a lot of ideas and was very supportive to the whole work. Likewise I had support from Lesley Hutchison, the RSC's Movement teacher at the time, who worked alongside and who contributed a great deal to the end result.

It was a great journey for me, to bring this huge play into existence: and I think I can say successfully so, for it went on to play at the Almeida Theatre in London, with some change of cast. And here it was nominated for the Evening Standard Award for Best Director – alongside William Gaskill, Sir Peter Hall, Garry Hines, Declan Donnellan, Adrian Noble and Trevor Nunn. (In the end it was Nick Hytner who was preferred. But at least there was a nomination.)

The following pieces are taken from reviews that we had during the run at the Almeida Theatre. I am adding them, I stress, not out of vanity, but in order to underline the point that the language of a play can be as active and exciting as the movement or the set. It is up to theatre to excite people with language, to make them want to talk and exchange ideas: that surely is our mission.

> 'The clarity of the whole production ensures that the words, simply spoken, explode like words in a combustion chamber.' John Peter

> 'The major point to be made is that this production brings a great play alive with such immediacy that one feels nothing

intervening between oneself and Shakespeare.'
Charles Osborne

'Richard Haddon Haines plays Lear as a vigorously genial
aristocrat who responds to his early grievances by erupting
into paroxysms of ineffectual wrath. The last of these
outbursts coincides with the storm, after which he reverts to
down-to-earth speech, as though the storm had been only a
fantasy. Throughout the show, abrupt descents from sustained
tone to conversational expression set the words on fire. And
when Haines and Amanda Root's Cordelia link arms and
set off for prison swapping cheerful matter-of-fact talk, the
spectator supplies the tears.' Irving Wardle

'And Patrick Miller's Fool, with clownish white make-up
superimposed on his black features, brings out not only the
character's astringency but also his overwhelming pity. It
is a stirring evening that proves several things: that great
plays currently work best in small spaces, that truth to
Shakespeare involves capturing precisely his antithetical
mixture of harshness and hope and that understanding what
you are saying is the key that unlocks Shakespearean word-
music. "Was this well spoken?" enquires Lear. Indeed it was.'
Michael Billington

One last word: to everyone's great sorrow, Richard Haddon Haines
died in 1990. I will always remember him for his truthful and haunt-
ing portrayal of King Lear.

INDEX

Note: numbers in bold refer to the texts used in the Workshop exercises.